writing with class

To Sue —
A dear, dear
friend... Hope
you enjoy it!
Helen

Stories and Poems By

Helen P. Bridge

Jenny Menning

Susan Joy Bellavance

Trudy Cohen

Roberta Baldwin Stoneman

Sally L. Wright

Joan Chandler

Illustrations by
Joan Chandler

With Deb McKew

Words in Play™ Writing Workshops

backchannel press

portsmouth. new hampshire

WRITING WITH CLASS

ISBN 13: 978-1-934582-32-9
LCCN: 2010915755

BACK CHANNEL PRESS
170 Mechanic Street
Portsmouth, NH 03801
www.backchannelpress.com

Permissions from the following publications for previously published works:
Kearsarge Magazine
Upper Valley Life
Here in Hanover
SooNipi Magazine

Cover layout by Roger Goode & The Proper Pup Studio
www.properpup.com

Design and page layout by Back Channel Press

Main illustrator: Joan Chandler

Special illustrator: Sara Tang

Back cover photograph: Lynn St. Louis
www.timelessalloccasion.com

Copy editors: Joan Chandler, Jenny Menning, Helen P. Bridge

Printed in the United States of America

This book is dedicated to the idea that
writing is not a solitary act.

thesaurus:

a treasure trove
of words

Contents

AN INTRODUCTION

by Deb McKew

Have you ever wondered? Of course you have. However, you may not have realized what a powerful tool wonderment can be. It is the beginning of all creative activity. When you allow yourself to wonder, you experience life in new ways. Words help capture those experiences.

The story of this book is a story about how a group of writers grew in their craft by having some serious fun with words.

Magic happens when creative spirits meet; these authors have laughed and cried (mostly laughed), argued over syntax and point of view, shared many a potluck breakfast, pushed each other through false starts and rough endings, and, over all, experienced the joys and pains of putting their hearts on the page. It is their stories that shape this mosaic of prose and poetry that you, possibly an aspiring writer yourself, hold in your hands.

This eclectic group of writers produced this anthology, including memoir, fiction, essays, children's stories, and poetry, in a workshop environment, writing with class. Each, in her own way, has embraced the one principle I stress in all my workshops: words make great playthings—there is an endless supply; they are free; and you can throw away the ones that don't work.

"In play" means the subject, usually a ball, has not gone out of bounds. But in my *Words in Play* workshops, there is no "out of bounds" and the play is always in progress. The human brain is hardwired to be inquisitive, to learn, and to solve problems through the creative process. Playing is our minds' way of reinforcing that there is no wrong way to spark an idea.

Writing is a journey that surprises, exhilarates, frightens, heals, and most of all, rewards both writer and reader. I love the look on a writer's face when she "gets it"—that moment of revelation when she comes to understand what it is she is trying to say. As the seven authors here have demonstrated, the creative process is indeed serious fun.

So, go ahead, play with words: experiment, take chances, explore your world, enter new worlds, open your perceptions, and engage your senses—after all, words are wonderful…

www.wordsinplay.net

ALL of the writing in this book was inspired by, critiqued in, or generated from the workshop classes.

Helen P. Bridge

FIND MY VOICE? *I CAN'T EVEN FIND MY PEN!*

I am a storyteller. My five children might interpret that phrase differently, but what I mean is: I love to regale my friends, and even casual acquaintances, with stories about my life's adventures, good and bad. Over the years, as I perfected my skill at storytelling, I heard the constant refrain from my various audiences, "Helen, you really ought to write a book." My husband finally said in desperation, "Helen, if you don't write that book, I'm going to."

Storytelling for me has been a rich tradition, but always an *oral* one. I am the eleventh child born to a poor, unhappy Ohio farm family. With no father on the scene as I grew up, I was the culmination (or is it the nadir?) of a Depression-era family farm disaster:

1

five girls, one boy, and five more girls So I learned perseverance early. I also learned that life presents choices, and I chose joyfulness. When I was 15, I heard my half-brother, Earl, sneer to my mother, "You know, Helen finds life so *exciting*." He meant it as a pejorative, but I took it at full measure—life *is* exciting.

The best part of that excitement is connecting with others, and I connected through storytelling. Despite my friends' urging to write my story, I wasn't interested in writing. I wanted to perform. Then, I was enticed by Deb McKew to join her writing workshop, *Words in Play*. Our group bonded immediately, and I now had a brand new audience for my stories. But they wouldn't let me *tell* them, I had to *write* them. And it was hard. To make stories come alive on the written page was scarier than a trip to the outhouse on a moonless night. It was an unfamiliar and uncharted course for me. My colleagues and our teacher have helped me tremendously in that process.

Now in my 80s, I am at last *writing* my stories (although, I secretly long for the next adventure or mishap to occur so I can add it to my story telling and, in due course, to my memoir).

Deb's Insights:

I met Helen in my book group, the summer of 1997. Every month for 14 years, she has amused this group with humorous tales of her life. It seems she has a Mary Poppins bag of material from which to draw; she revels in the telling of each story, down to the most hilarious details. No person or event in her life is spared; she finds the humor in even the darkest of subjects. Helen's youth was far from privileged, and she is no stranger to tragedy, yet at 83, she is living proof that experiencing a full and happy life is a matter of attitude. And one is never too young or too old to have a good time.

When I started teaching my workshops, I suggested Helen join, to preserve her stories for her family. She resisted—for several years. She kept on telling stories at book group, and you would think, after more than a decade, that we would have heard them all. But, they just kept coming. Finally, with much coaxing, she relented and joined the workshop. Nothing has been the same since, for Helen, or for the writing group!

Helen approaches writing with equal parts gusto and procrastination. She loves getting her stories on paper, she loves hearing feedback, and she loves discovering even more stories that she thought were forgotten. But, she needs nudging now and then, to sit down and write. She thrives in the writing group for just that support and encouragement.

The workshops are all about growing as writers. You can't grow if you don't share and experiment. Helen's oral storytelling is always very vivid – she uses much inflection, body language, and facial expression to recreate her life in anecdotal form for an audience. But, when it came to writing the words on a page, she tended to skim over the sensory details. One day in our workshop, as a writing exercise, I asked the class to revise one paragraph of Helen's story submission, *Born to Dance*, by incorporating sensory imagery. The results thrilled Helen; she finally understood the magic of the written word and she was eager to continue on. She still procrastinates, but we've gotten her to the point of nearly finishing her first book of memoirs entitled, *Beware: The Bridges are Out.*

BEWARE: THE BRIDGES ARE OUT

(Excerpts from Helen's memoir)

Born to Dance

My family moved into a nearby town from our farm in rural Ohio when I was nine years old. My grandmother was seriously ill and my mother had to take care of her. Moving day was the happiest of my life. Suddenly, I had neighbors. I had sidewalks. I had stores. Hallelujah! I had left the farm.

Ah, the bliss of those first few months in a new town. I loved third grade with its many students. My only classmates in the one-room school I had previously attended were two obnoxious boys. My first new friend in town was a girl named Mary Jane who lived up the street from my grandmother's. We walked home together and often played after school.

"I can't play today," she suddenly announced one afternoon.

"Why not?"

"Oh, I have my tap-dancing lesson." Now, I didn't quite know what tap dancing was, but I knew right then it was something I definitely wanted to do.

I rushed home to ask my mother, "Mom, Mom, can I take tap-dancing lessons?"

"No," she replied.

"Oh, please, please, can't I? I want to so much."

"We don't have money for that kind of foolishness, so don't ask me again."

I was crushed. Despite my begging and pleading, she didn't change her mind. With very little money and a strong religious fervor, my mother didn't tolerate much frivolity. And, during the Depression of the 1930s, tap dancing was very frivolous.

A week later when Mary Jane went to her dancing class, I secretly followed her. I wanted to know where these mysterious lessons took place. The next Saturday I went alone back to the dance teacher's house. With trembling hand, I knocked on the door.

The door opened, and there stood the most exotic creature I had ever seen. Although it was almost noon, the woman who appeared before me was wearing a slinky silk robe made of colors never seen on our farm. She had jet black hair, vivid red lips, a face layered with makeup, and a cigarette dangling between her painted nails. Nothing in my strict, puritanical childhood had prepared me for this. She was stunning.

"What do you want?" she growled in a husky voice.

"Do…do…you…you give dance lessons?"

"Yes. Why?"

"Well, I really, really want to learn how to tap dance."

"Fine," she said, "the lessons are $3 a week."

I blurted, "I don't have any money and my mom won't pay for them."

"Well, that's a problem, kiddo. Do you think there is any way you could earn some money?"

"Uh, well, uh, I did a lot of chores on the farm taking care of animals and stuff, so maybe I could do some work for you to pay for lessons," I offered.

She laughed, "Well, honey, this ain't no farm, but maybe you could help clean up after that animal I live with. So, come on in and let's talk."

Wide-eyed, I followed her inside, expecting to find a cat or a dog somewhere.

"I'm Mrs. Carpenter, by the way. And what's your name?

"Helen. Helen Polen."

She stood there and just looked at me. What she saw was a stocky, freckle-faced, red-headed little nine-year-old with a bad haircut, obviously done at home.

As I squirmed under her gaze, she finally said, "Okay, here's the deal. I'll give you dance lessons in exchange for your coming every Saturday morning to help with chores around the house. Stuff like doing the dishes, changing the bed, and some dusting and sweeping. Do you think you can handle that?"

"Oh, yes, yes," I replied, and we agreed I would start the following Saturday.

I rushed home to tell Mother the wonderful news, but she didn't think it was so wonderful. "Absolutely not," was her curt reply.

I cried, I begged, and I pleaded. When she realized I was going to work hard for those lessons, she finally relented; a strong work ethic was high on her list.

How I treasured those Saturdays. Mrs. Carpenter's house enticed me with the forbidden aromas of cigarettes and heavy perfume—smells I had never encountered before. She also laughed and joked a lot, something I rarely heard at my house. I didn't even mind the stacked-up dishes, the overflowing ashtrays, and the endless clutter. I was learning how to dance.

The year passed quickly as I worked on my dance steps in my borrowed tap shoes. Mrs. Carpenter even let me take them home to practice during the week. I drove my family crazy as I tapped up the stairs, down the halls, tap-tap-tap everywhere. "It's utter nonsense," my mother would complain every time I tapped by her, but she didn't interfere.

Midway through the year, Mrs. Carpenter added acrobatics to my routines. I learned how to do cartwheels, backbends, and splits. I was on my way.

Third grade ended, and on the first Saturday of the summer break I rushed to my dance teacher's house. As I was washing the day-old dishes, Mrs. Carpenter walked in. She crossed her arms, narrowed her eyes, clicked a scarlet nail to her teeth, and, looking me up and down, announced, "Helen, I think you are ready to perform in public."

My heart skipped a beat. "P-p-public? Where? When?"

Tap, tap, tap went her foot as she continued to look at me. "Oh," she said, "this hick town doesn't have a dance hall or a public stage, but they do have a County Fair."

"The County Fair!" I couldn't imagine a space to dance at the fair. All I had ever seen were carnival rides, game and food booths, barns for livestock, a building to show all the produce, jams, and quilts, and a grandstand to watch the animal judging, harness races, and ox-pulls. "Where would I dance?"

"Oh," Mrs. Carpenter replied, "we'll just take that old flatbed truck of Al's and drive it to the fair, park somewhere, hook up the old Victrola, put you and a couple of my other students up on the back and let you go to it. The people will love it. But, you will need a dance costume."

My heart sank. If my mother wouldn't pay for dance lessons, she'd never pay for such a thing as a *costume*. Although all my clothes were made-over hand-me-downs, I knew I would never persuade her to sew me one either. "I can't get a costume. I just know I can't," I replied as I fought back the tears.

"Not to worry," said Mrs. Carpenter. "We'll just see if we can't salvage something for you from one of my former students."

She dragged out an old trunk, and we scavenged through outfits made with sparkles, sequins, and some brightly-colored stretchy fabric. Each one seemed more glamorous than the last. Finally, my teacher found one she liked. "I think this one will do the trick. Let's give it a try."

I hastily took off my shorts, slid out of my shirt, and stepped into Heaven. The costume was fabulous. It was bright pink with silver sequins around the neck and on the cap sleeves. And it had ruffles in the back. I didn't notice the missing spangles, the stretched threads or the rather worn, tawdry look of it. To me, it was perfect.

Mrs. Carpenter told me to be ready by one o'clock on the following Saturday. She also said I didn't have to clean that day so I would be fresh and ready for my performance. The week seemed endless. Saturday morning, I put on my sequined leotard and covered it with my usual outfit of shorts and shirt. I did not dare show Mother that costume; she would never let me leave the house. I had told her our dance teacher was taking some of her students to the fair, but I'm not sure I told her we were going there to dance.

Trying to contain my nervous excitement, I went out to sit on the curb to wait for my life to begin. My heart leapt when I heard the wonderful clatter of the old truck as it rounded the corner. It eased up to the curb and came to a clanking stop. I jumped in back, squeezed in with the other girls, and our rusting, sputtering chariot wheezed its way to the local fairgrounds.

Mr. Carpenter bumped that banged-up truck around the fairway until he found a suitable parking space. Our dance teacher hurried us out of the back and told us to put on our tap shoes. With her shielding us from view, we took off our outer clothes and got ready to perform. Then she plugged in that beat-up Victrola and the three of us climbed up to the warped wooden boards of the old truck.

We stood, first on one foot and then the other, waiting to begin our routines as the redolent smells of the fair wafted over us. Cotton candy, hot dogs, and popcorn mingled with the all-too-familiar odors of the cow barns. Screams fell from the ferris wheel, drowning out the oom-pah-pah of the merry-go-round. Hawkers lured unsuspecting victims to their games of chance or cried, "Come see the fat man, our tattooed lady, and the magical snake charmer!" Then, our music started and we forgot all that as we began to dance. Slowly, people began to drift over to the truck. After all, it was free; in 1937, that was a plus.

The hot sun reddened my skin as I relentlessly tapped and twirled on those old boards that afternoon. I wanted it never to end. It was not quite the setting I had dreamed of, but it was grand. I was on stage.

That summer, we danced at several fairs and at a few Grange halls in the area. One memorable performance took place in a church, where three of us performed an interpretive dance to that dirge of a hymn, "The Old Rugged Cross." There we were: ten-year olds draped in pink, gauzy costumes with veils and scarves, pantomiming away to

> *"On a hill far away stood an old rugged cross, the emblem of suffering and shame; and I love that old cross where the dearest and best for a world of lost sinners was slain. So, I'll cherish the old rugged cross, till my trophies at last I lay down; I will cling to the old rugged cross and exchange it some day for a crown."*

We managed to shuffle, twirl, and act out all four verses plus the refrain.

Then my dance career took a giant leap forward. My teacher had arranged for me to dance solo at a nightclub located just across the county line. Our county was dry, and this place was often vilified from the pulpit of our Christian Church. That fact must have eluded my dance teacher. I didn't know much about "The Hoot Owl," but even I knew it was considered bad.

When Saturday night came, I didn't tell my mother where I was performing. If she wanted to think it was another rendition of "The Old Rugged Cross" in some out-of-the-way church, that was fine with me.

Mrs. Carpenter's car rattled into our driveway. "Hop in, we're late," she shouted, and away we went. When we pulled into what our minister always called "the house of the Devil," I saw a rather run-down, ramshackle building with light bulbs haphazardly spelling out "The Hoot Owl." She stopped the car, opened the door, grabbed my hand, and said, "Well, come on, Helen, we haven't got all night." I think she sensed that I was more than a little reluctant to enter that building. For all I knew, I would be struck dead when I stepped through the door. But I trusted Mrs. Carpenter to keep me safe.

Taking my hand, she pulled me inside. Still alive, I looked around but couldn't see much for the gloom. Mrs. Carpenter led me to the bathroom and told me to get into my costume and tap shoes. With chattering teeth, I pulled on my sequined costume, tied my dance shoes, and timidly stepped out into the room. The place had a musty, closed-up smell, and all I could see were whirls of smoke curling around the lights overhead. Loud laughter, the clinking of glasses and the thumping of the drummer assaulted my ears.

Mrs. Carpenter grabbed me and pushed me toward the stage, where a three-piece band was banging away. Squinting, I peered through the lights and smoke to see what was out there. Suddenly, I heard my name. One of the musicians announced, "Friends, we have a special surprise for you tonight. Helen Polen is going to perform for us, so put your hands together and give her a big *Hoot Owl* welcome."

The lights brightened even more as Mrs. Carpenter shoved me out to center stage. The band started playing, "East Side, West Side." With my heart pounding even louder than the band, I tentatively began to dance. I tapped. I did cartwheels, backbends, and splits while the band wailed behind me. The crowd laughed. They applauded. Then they threw money on stage. Startled, I stumbled, not sure what to do. The guy playing the piano came to my rescue and said, "Pick it up, kid, it's all yours." I was in Paradise.

Before Sunday school and church the next morning, I secretly counted my ill-gotten gains. Then I uttered a fervent prayer, "Please, dear God, get my dance teacher to sign me up for next Saturday night."

My euphoria was short-lived. On the way out of church, some old biddy pulled my mother aside and confronted her with, "Do you know where your daughter, Helen, was seen last night?"

Mother replied, "Well, she had a dance recital."

"Dance recital, my foot," muttered the old busybody. "She was seen dancing out at that *Hoot Owl Inn*. She was up there on stage tap-dancing and showing off in a skimpy little outfit in front of all those drunks. It was shameful, I tell you. Just shameful."

My mother was horrified. As a founding member of the Women's Christian Temperance Union, she could not believe a child of hers would darken the door of such an evil place. Certainly not her well-behaved 10-year-old. Dragging me away from the church, she demanded to know the truth. A lie flickered momentarily in my mind, but one look at her face and I knew I was in for it. So, I confessed. Despite my tearful begging, Mother marched me straight to my dance teacher's home (or, as she called it, "that hussy's house").

Banging on the door until a sleepy Mrs. Carpenter opened it, Mother demanded, "Did you take my daughter to the *Hoot Owl* last night to perform?"

Mrs. Carpenter shrugged, "Well, yes, and they loved her."

My dancing career ended right then and there.

Going Postal

The summer of 1943, I was 15 and bored. I longed for a real job, but all I could see in my future was the same old, same old: working on the farm, housecleaning, and babysitting. I craved excitement. Something new. Something different. I didn't quite know what, but I knew the small town where I lived definitely wouldn't provide it.

One June Saturday afternoon, as I sat swaying on the porch swing contemplating my dreary existence, a shiny Ford drove up the driveway, and my older half-brother, Earl, stepped out. This was a little strange, since he usually only appeared at our traditional Fourth of July family reunions. With barely a nod in my direction, he came up the steps. "Is Mother here?" he asked curtly.

"Yeah, I think she's in the kitchen."

A few minutes later, my mom came out to the porch with my half-brother in close attendance and said, "Helen, what do you think of the idea of going to live in Cleveland with Earl for the summer?"

I looked at them in amazement. I really didn't know my brother very well, as he was long gone by the time I was growing up. He never said much to me at any of the family get-togethers, so why would he want me to spend an entire summer with him? Mother continued, "He and Dot would like to have you help around the house and do some babysitting for them."

My spirits took a nose dive. Where was the excitement in that? I would be doing just what I had been doing for the past several summers. Even though they lived in a big city, I would probably never get to see it. I would be stuck at the house working. Then Earl said the magic words, "Oh, and by the way, Helen, I also have a job for you at my company, so you will just have to help at home some evenings and weekends."

Now, that piqued my interest. "What kind of job?"

"Mail girl. You know, collect the outgoing mail, process it, sort and distribute the incoming mail. Just the usual stuff," Earl replied.

It took me about five seconds to decide that living and working in a big city was far superior to spending three months in the little farming town of Carrollton, Ohio. I jumped up. "When do I start?"

"Monday," Earl replied.

I spent the next several hours going through my pitiful wardrobe, trying to decide what a real grown-up office worker would wear. What I finally packed fit into a single dilapidated suitcase my mother found in the attic.

The next morning Earl picked me up, and off we headed for what I hoped would be the biggest adventure of my life. On the two-hour drive to Cleveland, my half- brother spent the time laying down the ground rules for the summer. "First, do not address me by my first name at the office. Second, do not tell anyone we are related. Third, do not tell anyone your age since you don't have a work permit."

The list went on and on. I lost track. My mind was busily engaged in imagining all the wonderful things that were going to happen to me. I would worry about the rules later.

We arrived at my brother's house early Sunday afternoon. His wife, Dot, showed me to my room, re-introduced me to their two small children, and then said, "Helen, why don't you unpack, and then I'll talk to you about what I would like you to do around the house."

"Okay," I replied. Later, I tried my best to focus on her instructions, but my excitement proved too much. It was all a blur. I would just have to wing it.

After a restless night, I had a quick breakfast, and then my brother and I boarded the Rapid Transit in Shaker Heights, a suburb of Cleveland, to commute into the city. My heart pounded and my eyes swiveled furiously as I tried to take in all the sights and sounds of the city. Earl interrupted my delirium, "Now, Helen, do you remember the rules about your conduct at the office? And pay attention on this ride, because you will probably be commuting by yourself from now on."

I nodded, but I didn't really understand why it was so important that I not call him by his first name or let anyone know we were related. Unaware of such things as office politics or nepotism, I thought he was afraid I might embarrass him by acting like a country bumpkin. Well, I would show him just how sophisticated I could be.

I was dazzled by every sight, smell and sound when I stepped off the train. The terminal building astounded me. Shops and restaurants lined the concourse. There were moving steps; I had never before seen an escalator. I gaped and gawked until my brother suggested I rein in my enthusiasm a bit. I tried, but it was like harnessing a wild horse.

We finally arrived at the company where my brother was the comptroller. A subsidiary of Sealtest, this milk and ice cream producer sprawled over a city block. Following introductions to my office mates, my brother ushered me to my workspace, where a fellow worker was to teach me my duties.

The mail trucks delivered the mail twice a day to the mailroom located at the rear entrance of the building. The employees there took out the packages and brought everything else to the mail station on the second floor where I worked. My job was to sort, open if necessary, and then deliver the mail to the appropriate people or offices. As I delivered the incoming mail, I was also to pick up all outgoing mail, process it by putting it through the stamp machine with the proper postage, and send it down to the mailroom below to be collected by the mail trucks on their routine pickups.

It didn't take me long to get to know everyone on my route. I would stop to chat with people in the offices, flirt with the guys in the plant, and snitch a few samples of ice cream as I breezed along.

When I didn't have to rush home to babysit, I explored downtown Cleveland. There was so much to discover. Strolling through the department stores, I fantasized over the fabulous displays, and dreamily imagined wearing such beautiful apparel. Our little stores at home looked mighty shabby by comparison.

At work, I gradually made friends with some of the secretaries. This added a whole new dimension to my life. Their conversations were far more scintillating than those of my school chums. I tried very hard not to let my eyes widen or my jaw drop when they discussed boyfriends, dating, clothes, movies, and even husbands. It was very glamorous, and I desperately wanted to emulate them.

These new-found friends taught me how to wear makeup and how to dress. For the first time, I owned a "store-bought" dress. Each day, I could feel another layer of sophistication being added. I didn't realize just how successful I was at being a grown-up until one day at lunch, Jeanne turned to me and said, "Helen, how come you've never married?"

Having just finished my sophomore year in high school, it hadn't occurred to me. But I just shrugged and said, "Well, I guess I just haven't met the right man yet."

I never wanted this job to end. The thought of going back to my little hometown and resuming my former mundane existence totally depressed me. One Friday afternoon in mid-August, as I sat at my desk contemplating all this, the phone rang. The president's secretary, Jill, said he wanted to see me. I quickly walked to his office and was ushered right in.

"Helen, here's a letter I want you to send out special delivery. It is very important that it go out today," the president said.

"Not to worry," I replied and went back to my mail desk and my trusty Pitney-Bowes. I entered the required 3 cents postage, added the additional 15 cents for special delivery, made certain that the do-it-all machine stamped "Special Delivery" on the envelope and sent it down the chute to the mailroom below. I alerted the mailroom that I was sending a special delivery letter. In those days, the post office actually hand-delivered these letters, and I wanted to make certain it did not get overlooked. I then returned to processing the monthly milk bills before heading out for the weekend.

Monday morning, I arrived at my workspace prepared to begin another wonderful week. On my desk was a handwritten note addressed to me. It read, "Helen, I want to see you at once." It was signed by the president.

I entered his office with my biggest smile. "Good morning, Boss."

He glared at me, and in a voice that could freeze water said, "There's nothing good about it. You are fired. I want you to gather your personal possessions and leave this building immediately."

Flabbergasted, I asked, "But, why?"

"You don't have any idea, do you, of what you've done?" he growled.

I felt tears forming behind my eyes. I had never seen anyone so angry. "What did...did I do?"

"Do you remember the special delivery letter I asked you to send out last Friday for me?"

"Oh, yes, I did that. I'm sure."

"Well, you idiot, you also sent out all our monthly milk bills special delivery!"

I stared at him with gaining comprehension. I had not changed the postage machine back to its normal setting after that letter. "But, but," I stuttered, "wouldn't the people at the post office have known that I didn't mean for them all to go special delivery?"

"How would they know? They probably thought it was some kind of promotion. What do you think all those Mom-and-Pop shops, convenience stores, and grocers thought when they got their milk bill special delivery?"

"I'm s..s..sorry." The tears began to fall.

"Sorry doesn't even begin to cut it," he snapped. "Not only did our customers get wakened in the middle of the night to be handed their damned milk bills, but then they sent their payments *and* their cancellations to me *at home*. Also, I might add, by SPECIAL DELIVERY! My weekend was a nightmare. Now, get out."

Gulping back sobs, I ran to my desk, grabbed my belongings, and fled the building. On the bleakest day of my life, I took my beloved Rapid Transit back to my brother's house and tearfully waited for him to come home. I wanted to apologize and beg his forgiveness, but when he came through the door, his wrath was palpable.

"What the hell were you thinking?"

"It was a mistake," I cried. "I didn't mean to send those bills special delivery."

"Well, you did, and you caused one big screw-up. I want you to pack your bag and take the bus back to Carrollton tomorrow." Then, he added, "Thank God, we don't have the same last name; they don't know we're related."

Fired from my first job and sent home in disgrace. Not quite the ending I had dreamed about, but school began and life moved on. And there was a new boy in our junior class. That helped.

After that summer of '43, my brother never spoke to me about it again. In fact, he rarely spoke to me at all. I still regret that I didn't apologize to him. Also, I would have liked to have thanked him for that magical summer in the city. I treasure the memories. It has made a great cocktail party story for all my city friends.

He Loves Me

I woke up in a bad mood and was more than willing to share it. Entering the bathroom, I was assaulted by the overflowing clothes hamper. "What do these kids do? Manufacture dirty clothes just to irritate me?" I grumbled to myself. The sight of the mangled, uncapped toothpaste tube lying on the sink and the still-damp towels from the previous night's showers draped haphazardly over the racks only added fuel to my end-of-the-winter blahs. I longed to escape to some deserted South Seas island.

After giving the kids a wake-up call, I trudged downstairs to fix breakfast. The ominous cloud hovering over me must have been visible when they finally got to the dining room. I tried, but I couldn't pick a single fight. "Did you make your beds?" I growled. Five heads nodded in unison as they stared, fascinated, into their cereal bowls. "What about your teeth? Did you brush them?" Again, silent nodding. Their usual boisterous behavior was noticeably absent. Quickly finishing their juice and cereal, they fled to the comfort of their suddenly lovable teachers.

I stared into my second cup of coffee and mentally began listing my complaints. Into this morose reverie padded my unsuspecting husband. With his usual cheerful morning greeting, Charlie sat down and opened the morning paper. Begrudgingly, I poured him a cup of coffee. "I suppose you're going to want some juice, cereal or eggs, too."

Somewhat surprised by this query—since this was what he had been having for breakfast for the past fourteen years of our marriage—he quickly submerged himself in the day's news as he sipped his coffee.

Then the litany began. "I'm tired of being taken for granted around here. I get up and fix breakfast. Do dishes. Do laundry. Clean the house. Fix lunch. Iron. Get dinner. Do the dishes. Go to bed. Get up. Start the whole lousy routine all over again. And who cares? Who says thank you? Where's the glamour? The excitement? It's just the same old thing day after day. When do you say, 'Helen, I love you. You're beautiful. I adore you'? Do you ever hear the kids say, 'Thank you, Mommy,' or 'I love you'?"

If Charlie had learned one thing in law school, it was never to take an adversarial position with a lunatic. With a gentle smile, he went back upstairs, shaved and dressed, came back downstairs, tried to give me a kiss, and beat a hasty departure for the calm and quiet of his disorderly office.

I was miffed he didn't try to appease me. "Coward," I muttered to myself as he left the house.

Charlie called at 11:00. "How about coming downtown and letting me take you to lunch?" he asked, all sweetness and light.

I wasn't about to capitulate so easily. In a long-suffering voice, I said, "Oh, no, I have far too much work to do here."

After several attempts to change my mind, he asked if I was planning on coming to town any time that day. He'd done our taxes and needed my signature. I told him I was coming later in the day to do some work at the Dayton Council on World Affairs.

"Give me a call when you leave the house. I can meet you at the curb in front of our building. You can sign the papers in the car."

I called him at one o'clock. Fifteen minutes later, I drove up in front of his office building. A large crowd had gathered at the corner, and in their midst stood my husband, literally buried under a dozen or more bouquets, some spilling out of his arms to the sidewalk. I pulled over to the curb, and when I rolled down the window, Charlie began to toss the flowers into the car. "I love you. I love you. I love you," he shouted. The assembled crowd cheered and applauded.

"What are you doing, you fool? You're making a scene," I cried. "Just give me the paper to sign."

Inundated by flowers, I pulled away from the curb to leave this maniac, who was now throwing me kisses and crying, "I adore you, I adore you," and wiping the tears from his eyes as I departed.

When I walked into the Council office, the receptionist was on the phone saying, "I'm sorry, but Mrs. Bridge isn't here right now. Oh, just a moment, she just walked in." She handed me the phone.

"Well, who would know that I was going to be here?" I asked. "Hello, this is Helen Bridge."

"I love you. I miss you. You're wonderful."

I shrieked and nearly dropped the phone. "All right, Charlie, I give up. Enough is enough." Then I laughed, and laughed some more.

Five times he called me that afternoon, each time with a new expression of love and appreciation. Later, I drove home chuckling to myself about the nut I had married and feeling a little chagrined by my morning's behavior. Ah, but the game wasn't over yet.

As I pulled into our driveway, I saw Charlie standing there with a big smile on his face, and our kids waving hastily scrawled signs saying, "We love you! We love you!" Charlie also held a sign, one proclaiming, "I love you" in big block letters.

They all clamored around me, singing my praises. I cried, "Uncle," and promised I would never complain again. A promise which, of course, I didn't keep.

After dinner, I told Charlie I had to deliver some material to a woman who had requested it from the World Affairs office that afternoon. I drove to her house and knocked on her door. She thanked me profusely for delivering the booklets so promptly, and as I was heading back to my car, she called, "Oh, by the way, Mrs. Bridge, your husband just called and asked me to tell you he loves you."

A reporter heard about the day's events and wrote a story for our local paper; the headline blared, "There's Only One Way to Convince a Redhead." In the article, he quoted the flower vendor as saying, "Best d----d day I ever had!" And you know, I felt the same way.

Where's Eb?

Okay, so maybe I will never win the *Mother of the Year* award. I love my children dearly, but I have to admit, there were times when the child welfare people probably could have made a good case for intervention. In my defense, there were extenuating circumstances, namely, rearing five children (at one point, four of them were under the age of 6). I rest my case.

For starters, let me tell you about my third child. Eb is a wanderer. He started at a very young age and has perfected his skill at disappearing to a fine art. Even today, some 50 years later, he can vanish in an instant. You can be talking to him, turn away for one second, turn back, find he's gone, and you haven't a clue as to where he went. He constantly amazes guests and relatives. The resounding cry in our household has, and always will be, "Where's Eb?"

It all started in Oakwood, Ohio, where we lived during our children's growing-up years. My husband and I felt that this small town, a bedroom community of Dayton, was the perfect place for kids: good schools within walking distance; houses close together on tree-shaded streets and boulevards; and neighbors with lots of children.

Eb started his disappearing act at age 2. By the time he reached kindergarten, everyone who lived on all sides of our block knew Eb, as they had participated in countless searches for him. The call would go out, "Where's Eb?" or "Eb's missing!" and the hunt would begin.

Sometimes, I didn't even know he was missing until I received a phone call, or he would be delivered somewhat unceremoniously to our front door. I recall one particular Saturday evening when Eb was about four. I was busy fixing dinner when the phone rang. Wasting no time with pleasantries, my neighbor, who lived several houses away barked, "Helen, it's Lucia. Would you please come get this kid of yours, right now?"

When I retrieved Eb, I learned that Lucia had been luxuriating in a quiet bath, in the privacy of her own bathroom, when the door opened and in walked Eb, thumb in mouth and the ever-present "blankie" trailing behind him. He solemnly surveyed the scene while Lucia shrieked.

Eb's first walkabout began at age two. It began with Agnes. A woman in her late eighties and extremely deaf, Agnes was a dear friend of my husband's. She lived in a small town about twenty-five miles south of us. In mid-March, we spent a delightful evening with her, and while there, Agnes remarked, "Oh, Helen, do you know they've just released the movie *Singing in the Rain* with Gene Kelly. I so want to see it."

Knowing she couldn't go by herself and thinking the movie wouldn't arrive in Dayton for several weeks, I graciously replied, "Agnes, I would be delighted to take you to the movie when it comes to Dayton."

Two weeks later, I gave birth to my fourth child, Tommy. Exactly two weeks after that, I got an early morning phone call from Agnes. "Helen," she said, *Singing in the Rain* is at the Loew's, and I have a driver who will bring me to your house today and then take us to the 2 p.m. matinee. Isn't that wonderful?" Obviously, this was a woman who never had children.

Stunned, I tried to explain. "Oh, Agnes, I have a brand new baby, and I don't have a sitter, so I don't know how I could go today. Perhaps next week would be better."

Deaf Agnes responded, "Yes, Helen, you better get a sitter." She obviously didn't hear any of the words between "sitter" and "better."

I struggled once more to explain my predicament, but failed miserably. Agnes cheerily replied, "Okay, Helen, I'll see you at one o'clock," and hung up!

Frantically, I began calling sitters. None of my regulars was available, so I resorted to a sitter service that I had never used. The woman called me back and said she had found a college girl who was available. I called the young girl immediately and gave her directions to our house.

My two older children came home for lunch. I fed them and hurried them back to school. I put Eb in his crib for his afternoon nap and dressed for the movie. The phone rang. I prayed it was Agnes saying she couldn't come, but it was the sitter. "Oh, Mrs. Bridge, my car won't start. Can you pick me up?" I thought about a cab, but I knew there wasn't time. When I found that she only lived a short distance away, I agreed to go get her.

I looked in on Eb. He was fast asleep. I knew that if I woke him up to go with me, I would never get him back down for his nap. Since I was only going to be gone less than 10 minutes, I left him sleeping. Grabbing Tommy in his bassinet, I carried it to the car and drove to the sitter's.

Arriving back at our house, I sensed the sitter's nervousness with a new baby. Fortunately, I had a little time before Agnes was due to give detailed instructions. "Tommy will probably want to be fed at about 2:00 or 3:00 p.m." I showed her how to warm the bottle and test a drop on her arm to make certain it wasn't too hot, and how to burp the baby. Then I said, "Now, my 2-year-old, Eb, is asleep upstairs in his crib. When he wakes up, you'll need to change his diaper and put on the clothes I left on the changing table for him. You can give him some juice and a graham cracker for a snack. My 5 and 6-year-old children, David and Debby, will be home about 4:00, and they can have some juice and crackers, too." The sitter looked dazed.

Agnes arrived. With more than a little trepidation, I headed out the door. Just as I was about to step into Agnes' car, I saw our school principal's sister, who lived on the next block, coming towards me. Shock riveted me motionless; the woman was carrying my Eb, barefoot and clad only in a diaper. I stared in disbelief. "Helen, do you know who this child belongs to? I found him wandering down our sidewalk dressed like this in the middle of April," she blustered.

I managed to reply, "Oh, Margaret, I do know where he lives. I'll be glad to take him to his house." I may have been stunned, but I wasn't totally witless.

She muttered something more about the irresponsibility of parents and stuff like that, but I was too busy thinking, "If that kid calls me Mommy, I'll strangle him." My next thought was "How did he get out of his crib, come downstairs, open the door and escape—all in the short time I was gone?" I didn't even know he could escape from his crib.

Thank goodness Agnes seemed totally oblivious to the utter chaos around her. I rushed Eb inside, put him back to bed, and made certain he was warmly covered. I didn't give much of an explanation to the sitter. She looked even more alarmed.

We arrived at the theater and settled in our seats. The lights dimmed and the movie screen came alive, and I got the shakes. Gene Kelly may have had wonderful feelings while singing and dancing in the rain, but I was suffering the agonies of the damned. I thought of all the things that could have happened. Eb could have been hit by a car, while crossing the street. He might not have been seen, and wandered alone for hours before he succumbed to hypothermia. If we had left the house two seconds earlier, the sitter wouldn't have known Eb belonged to me. She thought he was sleeping peacefully in his crib. Poor Margaret would have wandered up and down the street trying to find the child's mother. Or, Eb could have said "Mommy." Then Margaret would have told her sister, the school principal, who would surely have reported me to the child welfare people. Would they have taken my children from me? Could I be sent to jail for child abandonment? My husband would have to give up his law practice and we would have to sell our house, at a loss of course, and move away. While Gene just kept splashing about in all that water, I saw my whole life going down the drain.

Elocution

From the moment I had my first elocution lesson at age 10, I was hooked. I discovered very early the heady thrill of public speaking.

During my grade school and high school years, I performed whenever and wherever possible. I entered speech contests. I gave poetry and prose readings. I was invited to recite "The Gettysburg Address" on Memorial Day following a big parade to the local cemetery. I joined the debate team and the drama club. I loved being on stage.

In college, I majored in speech and journalism. I saw myself as the next Pauline Fredericks reporting from the United Nations, or the female equivalent of Edward R. Murrow. I never considered the written word. It was the spoken word that seduced me. I didn't want to write—I wanted to perform.

My life didn't turn out the way I had visualized. Following college and a brief career that included some public speaking, I married and started a family. However, I joined the Speaker's Bureau of the League of Women Voters and the Council on World Affairs, so I was able to continue public speaking.

At first, the main focus of my talks was the United Nations—its purpose, functions, and weaknesses. Gradually, I began to broaden my topics. Program chairmen were desperate. Once, I was asked to speak on women's labor problems around the world. I was never quite sure whether I was supposed to talk about childbirth or the labor market.

Then the problems began. My husband, Charlie, had a notion that anyone who spoke in public should be fully conversant with the topic. In fact, he thought one should be an expert in the field. I held a different view. Anyone could speak on any subject, provided he or she did the necessary research. "After all," I told him, "a person's attention span is about five minutes. It's not what you say but how you say it."

Charlie was not one to capitulate easily. When his requests, admonitions, and, finally, pleadings failed to deter me from accepting speaking engagements, he resorted to dirty, under-handed sabotage.

One evening, as he was lying on the sofa buried in *The New York Times*, I casually asked what he knew about peace-time uses of atomic energy. "Absolutely nothing," he replied. A few minutes passed. Then he asked in a stricken voice, "Why?"

"Oh, I have to give a talk on the subject at the YWCA next week and I thought you could save me a trip to the library." I won't repeat what he said, but he voiced strong objections to my presenting on a subject I knew little about.

If he thought that was going to stop me, he certainly had learned little from our years together. Ignoring his complaints, I checked out all the books and articles on the subject from our local library. I drafted my speech and began to rehearse it.

The day before my appearance at the "Y," I received a phone call.

"May I speak to Mrs. Bridge?"

"Speaking," I answered.

"Mrs. Bridge, this is Florence Kelly, secretary to Mr. Howard George, whom you know is the regional vice-president of General Electric."

My first thought was that I hadn't paid the electric bill. But I didn't think vice-presidents called for that. I said in an assured voice, "Oh, yes, of course."

"As you also must know, Mrs. Bridge, General Electric is heavily involved in atomic energy research."

There it was, the red flag, but I was too involved in sounding all-knowing to notice it. I didn't say I was smart – just enthusiastic.

I cleared my throat. "Yes, of course."

"Mrs. Bridge," Miss Kelly went on, "General Electric is planning a tri-state regional meeting next month to which all of our top-flight engineers will be invited. The entire conference is to be devoted to peace-time uses of atomic energy. Mrs. Bridge, Mr. George wants you to be our keynote speaker."

I could only stare at the phone. After a few ahs, ohs, and uhs, I finally found my voice and responded weakly, "Oh, Miss Kelly, I don't believe I could speak to such a...ah...knowledgeable group."

After all, even I had limitations. Miss Kelly mercilessly persevered.

"I'm sorry, but have I got the right Mrs. Bridge? Mrs. Charles Bridge?"

What could I say?

"Well, I just don't understand," she purred. "Your name was given to us by a leading authority as someone deeply interested in atomic research. In fact, are you not speaking on the subject this week?"

I was trapped. "Oh, I really don't believe that my talk...uh...oh...would satisfy the kind of technical minds your engineers have. I intend to just give a very broad overview of the topic."

"Oh, Mrs. Bridge, that's just what we had in mind. We want to begin the conference with the broad picture, and then spend the remaining time in small group discussions going into more detailed and technical matters of atomic energy research."

I gulped.

"Miss Kelly, I am flattered to be asked to speak to such a distinguished gathering, but I must decline. My interest in atomic energy, and particularly its peace-time uses, has been long standing." (I wasn't going down without some pride intact.) "However," I continued, "my research, extensive as it is, has not prepared me to speak to men who are devoting their lives to researching ways that this awesome and destructive power can be harnessed. Rather I should listen to THEM. I'd be honored to attend your opening session and listen and learn from one of your top engineers giving the keynote address."

I smiled a little smugly, thinking how well I had handled the situation. But I was not to be let off so easily. At this point I heard my husband's voice on his secretary's extension say, "Well, thank God, you DO have some limits."

Shaken, but undeterred, I gave my speech the next day. As I warmed to my topic, my confidence returned and I ended on a rousing note of optimism about the marvelous energy resource that was about to be ours. I sat down to a comforting round of applause. Then I got carried away. I offered to answer any questions that my audience might have.

A little old lady in the back of the room tentatively held up her hand. Encouragingly, I said, "Yes?"

"Oh, Mrs. Bridge, I so enjoyed your talk, but you know I just never did understand Einstein's theory of relativity. Would you be so kind as to take a few minutes to explain it to all of us?"

I have always wondered how much that cost Charlie – or maybe it *was* Charlie in drag!

The Dating Game

I hated paying insurance bills. My philosophy was that you only spent money on food, clothing, shelter and fun. Each time I complained, my husband, Charlie, would patiently remind me, "Helen, it's the only way I can build a nest egg for you and the children in case something happens to me."

"Ha." I scoffed. "Honey, if anything happens to you there are plenty of guys out there just waiting in line." After Charlie's untimely death, I often recalled those innocent conversations and my cavalier response. The doorbell never rang. I didn't see a single queue anywhere. I know Charlie was secretly snickering somewhere.

After a couple of years alone, I began to think how nice it would be to have an escort. The thought of re-entering the dating scene in my forties, however, was daunting. Adding my five children to the dating experience was downright scary. Fortunately, I didn't have to worry. The doorbell still had not rung.

Finally, my thirteen-year old son, Tom, decided it was time that I met someone. And he had just the person in mind. His widowed Boys' Choir director. He began his campaign. "Hey, Mom, why don't you come to rehearsal tonight?" Then, "Mom, will you take charge of the candy sales?" or "Could you drive some of us to our next concert?"

Meanwhile, he was dropping not-too-subtle hints to his director, Paul, that I, too, was single and lonely. Surrendering to my son's relentless efforts, Paul finally called me, "Helen, Tom thinks we should...uh...I mean I was wondering if you would like to go out to dinner with me next Saturday night."

What could I say except, "Why that sounds great. I would love to."

The evening of the big date arrived. While I was getting ready, Tom nearly drove me nuts. He kept popping upstairs to see how I was doing. When I finally managed to get dressed, he gasped, "You're not going to wear that?" Great for confidence building. His next bit of advice was, "Now, Mom, please don't queer it and sing." This to a woman who is tone deaf. A woman to whom he had pleaded with hands covering his ears, "Don't song me, Mommy, don't song me," as she gently rocked him to sleep. The vision of me suddenly bursting into "Some Enchanted Evening" during dinner at the restaurant became more memorable than the date.

Paul and I managed to get through the evening without song. Arriving home later, he walked me to my front door. As I turned to say good night and considered whether a kiss was in order, the door burst open, and in the sudden brilliance of the flooding light, there stood my son. "What are you doing? Why are you standing out here?" Tom cried. A thirteen-year-old chaperone was just what I didn't need.

Despite my son's best efforts, Paul and I did not make music together. Tom still thinks I sang.

My next suitor was the minister of our church. William had been widowed for about a year. One night after a board meeting, he said "Helen, would you mind stopping by my office before you leave?"

Assuming it was a business matter, I said, "Sure." I was truly flustered when he asked me if I would like to go out with him. Having grown up in a fundamentalist church, I viewed our minister as a close second to God. Besides, I was socially uncomfortable with men of the cloth, worried that an occasional "damn" or "hell" would sneak out. Perhaps I feared being judged and found wanting.

I didn't quite know how to say "no," so I accepted. The evening went well and we went out a couple more times, but I was always on guard. Bill, however, was not. As my kids would say, "He came on like gangbusters."

A little overwhelmed by his amorous attention, I was more than happy to put some time and distance between us as I left Ohio and headed to New Hampshire for the summer. Then, one day in early July, Bill called. He just "happened to be in the neighborhood" and "could he possibly come to visit for a few days?" How could I reasonably refuse? I invited him for the Fourth of July weekend. Thank goodness our traditional family get-together included my kids and all of the nearby relatives. There's safety in numbers.

It was an eye-opening experience for my children. I spent the weekend intercepting passes, avoiding close encounters, and leaping up the minute Bill sat down next to me.

My nieces and nephews at the party still talk about my minister friend and his "tactile" pursuit. My kids kept murmuring to each other, "This is *our* mother and he is *our* minister."

Years later, my youngest son, Doug, gave an account of this dating experience to amused family and friends, summing it up beautifully with "I finally learned what *laying on of the hands* really means."

Next was Bernie. Bernie was the entertainment writer for the local newspaper. He reviewed theater, restaurants, night clubs, and visiting entertainers. He also had quite a reputation as a womanizer, with a string of marriages and affairs behind him. Therefore, I didn't pay much attention to him when I met him at a party. Maybe that was what intrigued him.

About a week after that party, he called me. "Hi, Helen, it's Bernie. There's a new show coming to Suttmiller's this week, and I wondered if you'd be my date for opening night?"

My first thought was, "Omigod, what will the children think?" My second was "Hey, what the heck, why not? It might be fun." So, I accepted.

The night of our date, Bernie jauntily drove into our driveway in a little Lotus Europa. Doug rushed out of the house ahead of me to get a closer look at this snazzy British sports car. When Bernie said, "Hop in, kid, I'll take you for a spin," I knew my youngest was sold on this suitor.

Bernie was fun, exciting, and manic. We met celebrities when they came to town. We were invited to fancy soirees. We wined and dined at the very best places. He also wisely involved my kids in these activities. He wooed them as much as he did me. I reminded myself, however, that he was far too unstable for any permanent relationship.

We had been dating for about two months when Thanksgiving rolled around. To celebrate, Bernie took us all out to dinner. Between the entrée and dessert, he lifted his champagne glass and announced to my children, "Listen up, you Bridge kids. I am going to marry your mother." That was news to me. I hadn't even been asked. Later, I assured my kids it wasn't going to happen, much as they liked that Lotus.

Christmas came and all the kids were home again from school. We made plans to include Bernie in our traditional family dinner. He canceled, but I didn't think too much of it. I knew he was busy.

Shortly after New Year's, Bernie was a no-show for a party we'd planned to attend together. I called him at home and at the newspaper. There was no answer. The next day, I called again. His receptionist said, "I'm sorry, but Bernie has told me not to accept any calls from you." That's how it ended.

I did my best to explain to my youngest what had happened. "I'll live through it," I told him. "I'm not the first one Bernie threw overboard."

Startled, Doug asked, "Did any of the others drown?"

A dozen years passed, and I decided I was destined to be single. I missed having someone with whom to share my life, but I accepted it and moved on. Then I met John.

John served on a volunteer fundraising committee for the Dartmouth Medical School, and I was the staff officer. After a couple of years of working together, we scheduled some "business" lunches to plan a campaign strategy for Vermont, John's home state. It didn't take long for those lunches to become dinners. Both widowed and ready for some fun and companionship, we began dating. Before long, it was time to introduce him to my children.

I invited John to join us for an informal Sunday cookout at our summer home where my children were vacationing. When he arrived, the kids were sprawled on the sun porch in casual cutoff jeans and khakis. They looked a little alarmed at John's bright, lime green pants and crisp pink shirt—colors my kids obviously weren't used to seeing. When I introduced him to my youngest, Doug inquired, "Where in nature do you find those colors?" Oh, we were off to a fine start.

John good-naturedly joined in the laughter and things seemed to be going along well. Then it came time to grill the meat. We were having a butterflied leg of lamb, which I had prepared many times before. John gallantly offered to do the grilling. I accepted.

When the coals were ready, I brought out the lamb, which had been marinating in oil, wine, and herbs. As I watched, John proceeded to bank the coals to the side of the Weber grill, planning to roast the lamb by the convection method. I hastily intervened, "Oh, no, you spread the coals and put the lamb on top. You grill it, not roast it."

John cajoled, "Now, Helen, I've cooked lamb many times before and the way to do it is with the coals off-side."

With clenched teeth, I replied sweetly, "No, John, trust me on this. You grill the lamb, just like a steak."

The children, sitting on the porch observing this polite bickering, secretly flashed the "thumbs down" sign to one another. David whispered to Tom, "He's history."

Eb said to Debby, "Don't even bother to learn his last name. He's out of here."

Meanwhile, I was losing what little patience I had. It was *my* dinner, *my* lamb, and I was damned well going to grill it, not roast it. After a few more attempts to persuade John that my way was best, I lost it. I just spread the coals and slammed the leg of lamb on top of the grill. The marinade erupted and splattered all over John's lime green pants. I was mortified, but John kept his cool. I apologized profusely and rushed for the spot remover. Nothing worked. Those spots were there to stay.

We managed to get through dinner with the "grilled" leg of lamb and John went home. Critiquing him, my kids all agreed he had handled my little tantrum with decorum. I spent the better part of the following week shopping for a new pair of lime green pants. To my utter amazement, I actually found a store that sold them.

Years later, John finally confessed. "Helen, I never cooked lamb on a grill before, but after all the instructions and directions from you and your kids, I just decided it was time to assert myself."

John still has his lime green pants and he refuses to part with them. He and the pants proved to be keepers.

An excerpt of Helen's memoir has been published in *Kearsarge Magazine*. Her favorite authors include Ernest Hemingway, Willa Cather, Wallace Stegner, Penelope Lively, Ivan Doig, Alice Munro, and Ian McEwan. (It was tough for her to narrow the list down to just these few!)

Invitation to Play

ThePrompt

Helen spends her summers in an historic home on Lake Sunapee in New Hampshire. She generously offers it as a place for us to gather and write; she has even hosted one of my weekend retreats at this special site. Named Sommerro House (Summer's Rest), the house has provided much inspiration to our writing group; stories fill every corner. One day, I offered the following prompt to the group and let them loose in the house to write for 15 minutes. Here is Helen's unedited response to the prompt:

The Clock Winked

*The clock winked…*as it merrily ticked away the minutes. Somehow, it knew that I was procrastinating and this was its gentle reminder for me to get started. I looked at the silver teapot. All these possessions that I have to sell, or give away. My house has been sold and I am moving to a much smaller place with no room for all these things I have accumulated over the years. But how to you give away memories? If that teapot is no longer there, will I still be able to see my mother pouring tea for her ladies' group? Will I still see her hands or the look on her face as she so graciously filled the cups? What is it about possessions? They clutter your home, your life, and your mind. But they are also reminders. They nudge your brain to recall that favorite time, that trip you took, what your husband said when he gave you that gift. Or, the look on your children's faces when you opened their presents. These objects all tell a story. Sometimes they are happy stories, and sometimes they are sad. But they are the story of your life, and now I have to part with them. My mind has already begun its slow pace of forgetfulness, so how can I hold fast to my past if I have to give up my reminders? All these triggers to my memory that jolt me awake just like that little winking clock. Perhaps, I could keep the teapot and fill it full with all the memories that each precious possession imparts. That way I will only have one thing to keep, rather than all these countless other things. Yes, that is what I will do. As I rid myself of each item, I will recall its memory and put it in the teapot. Then, when I am alone in my new home, I can open the lid and slowly begin to remember. I winked back at that little clock, and said, "Yes, that's what I am going to do."

The Prompt:

Choose a word blindly from a box and, for each of the following prompts, write using that word as inspiration (3 minutes for each). Helen chose the word "onions" and these are her responses (unedited):

Onions

Describe what it is:

All onions are not alike. Some are small bulbs called shallots. Some are white with long green stems. Those are scallions. Then there is the purplish Bermuda onion, and the sweet Vidalia onion. But my favorite is the Spanish onion. When I first saw their bright green shoots for mile after mile growing out of the black volcanic ash of Lanzarote, I was hooked. Their taste is similar to a Vidalia, but not as sweet. More spicy and pungent.

Write to Convince others:

Onions have a bad rap. They make you cry when you cut them. They stink up your kitchen when you cook them. But you haven't lived until you have tasted a sweet Vidalia onion or a spicy Spanish one. The Vidalia has an aroma that entices. Baked, it is ambrosia. Slices on a hamburger please the palate and enhance the lowly burger. Onions add zest and flavor to cooking. Without them your food is blah and uninteresting.

Write for yourself:

I love cooking with onions. Even the ones that make you cry when peeling them. I've tried all kinds of techniques to keep the tears from flowing: bread held between your teeth while peeling them: keeping your eyes closed, although that's risky; peeling them under running water; and even wearing special glasses. But, I still cry. However, the zest the onion brings to my cooking is well worth a few tears. They enhance my meals.

Write to Connect people:

The onion fields of Lanzarote were fascinating. I was visiting my former boss and his wife who were living there. Driving over the barren landscape that looked like the surface of the moon, I was mesmerized. As my boss, Curtis probably had the most influence on my early life. He was single when I first met him and we had a mild romantic fling, but it ended when he told me he was engaged. But he was to become my teacher, my mentor, and my role model. Following their marriage, he and Dorothy became my dearest friends, and we shared many adventures together. The onions of Lanzarote brought us together once more.

Write to teach others:

Just as all onions are not alike, so are we as human beings. We come in all shapes, sizes, and colors. We bring different flavors to each other's lives. We can enrich our own life experiences and other's just as the onion adds zest to the stew. We should rejoice in our differences and take pride in our uniqueness. Just as the onion is an indispensable ingredient for flavoring our food, we can be that indispensable ingredient for enriching our lives as well as others'.

Write to vent:

Sometimes, I feel just like the lowly onion. I am not a standout. I am way down on the beauty list. Compared to lovely green asparagus or elegant purple eggplants, the onion is downright plain in appearance. I can relate to that. I aspire to be something else – to be thinner, or younger, or prettier. Even though I console myself with the thought that I have served a good purpose in my life just like the onion, it is sometimes difficult. Then I think of the zest and flavor the onion has brought to our palates and I feel better. We are indispensable.

The Prompt:

Writing a list is one of my favorite ways to stimulate the creative juices. For this prompt, I asked writers to write a list of everyday household chores, then to choose one and just write. (10 minutes) Here is Helen's response:

Laundry Days

The smell of freshly laundered clothes entices me to this day. Especially if they have been hung outdoors. The fresh, crisp, clean air lingers on each piece of clothing as I fold it into my laundry basket. Instantly, my mind travels back to a time long past, when I was a small child living on a farm. I loved laundry days. As my mother hung the sheets on the line, I would run among them playing hide and seek. She would scold me if I dared to touch them, or kick up dirt on any of the clothes. I can see the shirts and overalls as they flapped and danced in the breeze, as if eager to get back to their farm chores. I recall clothes hung out in the dead of winter, freezing stiff as the icicles hanging from the roof, then carried into the kitchen to thaw on racks by the wood stove. In later life, I always wondered why the clothes had to go through the baptism of freezing cold before being brought inside. I never asked my mother that question. In fact, there are so many questions I didn't ask. And now, it's too late. So many times, we are transported back to our childhood by the touch of something cherished and long forgotten. The faded photograph. The smell of something instantly recognizable from the past. I feel my life has come full circle, but where and when did the circle start?

Jenny Menning

AMERICAN FARE: A SLICE OF LIFE, WITH A SIDE OF HUMOR

About thirty years ago, as a college student, I gave up the pursuit of a chemistry degree, opting instead for English. Three jobs, four houses, a husband and two kids later, I'd amassed enough life experience to feel the need to record some of the most humorous and memorable moments of my past.

In March, 2005, I joined a creative writing class instructed by Deb McKew, and have taken part in her *Words in Play* workshops ever since. I've tried my hand at personal essays, poetry, and short fiction. The next step: a novel?

I've learned that free writing captures inspiration, editing requires determination, and deadlines elicit perspiration. I've also learned that the structure and camaraderie in our writing group helps me overcome the most difficult part, for me, of being a writer…discipline.

An English degree comes in handy if you want to be a writer, but now I've discovered that there's also a chemistry to writing creatively:

- Study the elements of a good story

- Combine true life events with some fictional concoctions

- Stir in some humor

- Mix well with a trusted writing group who will critique, clarify, and distill your formula

- Then, adjust your glasses, stand back, and bubble over with the satisfaction that comes from creating your own composition

Deb's Insights:

Jenny joined my very first creative writing workshop, an adult education evening course. She registered herself and her then 13-year-old daughter, so they would have an activity to share. Her daughter appeared on the first night and then opted out; Jenny stayed.

Jenny approached storytelling as many new writers do. She wrote about the characters who populated her world—her family, her friends, her dog—and the shining moments that stood out to her. She recounted her youthful days in rural Ohio, the early years of her marriage, and the slapstick kinds of incidents she got herself into. Some of these tales seemed too comical to be true. Yet, all were real life, and heartfelt.

As she became more confident in the craft, she started fictionalizing her stories; she began to add the hyperbole, one dash at a time. Then, she had a breakthrough. For a class assignment, she wrote a story called *Black Magic* about Halloween, her favorite holiday. The piece was published in a local magazine. This encouraged her to keep writing. Another class assignment, a personal essay she wrote about frugality, was published in *New Hampshire Magazine*.

Getting published isn't Jenny's prime motivation. With each piece she writes, she explores and discovers something about herself; it isn't just about the memories rattling around in the recesses of her mind, it is about what those memories might mean: what is the bigger truth of those moments she is reliving on the page? What is her understory? She has figured out that writing fiction is a way for her to uncover what she feels and understands about the events and people that have shaped her. Jenny has learned what makes a good story good, and is now able to translate her life experiences into stories on a page. She's also having a whole lot of fun in the process.

IF IT'S TUESDAY, THIS MUST BE RUDY

Whether or not you're interested in politics, you probably couldn't help noticing that the 2008 presidential election campaign was one of extraordinary proportions. A wide field of candidates sparked enthusiasm early in the running, and a tight race between front-runners, in both the Democratic and Republican parties, lent an extra level of excitement in primary elections all across the United States. This election marked the first time in 56 years in which neither an incumbent president nor a vice president ran for re-election. And, more than 56 percent of the voter population turned out to cast their votes—the highest in 40 years. What an historic presidential race, and it all began with New Hampshire's "First-in-the-Nation" primary...

The invasion of the presidential candidates enthralled me during the autumn and winter of 2007. They arrived by mail, by telephone, by television, and by Internet. For weeks, I was doused in debates, interrogated by opinion pollsters, and pummeled with political propaganda. I received 13 glossy, full-color, tri-fold advertisements from one candidate alone. My e-mail inbox was clogged with humorous, nasty, and often erroneous political jokes, and campaign signs sprouted out of snow banks where our rural byways met the interstate. Was I irritated by all of this inundation? Absolutely not! The countdown was on for the New Hampshire primary, and I answered the charge with an enthusiastic, "Bring it on!"

New Hampshire's distinction of holding the country's first primary is a source of pride for its citizens, who clamor to be among the earliest voters to have our say. And, the presidential hopefuls woo those voters in highly publicized events, attempting to capture that all-important momentum. In the first week of 2008, during that sweet, short period of time between the Iowa caucuses on January 3rd and the New Hampshire primary on January 8th, all the candidates descended upon the Granite State in force. Yes, they were coming to *my* state—to see *me*.

I called my friend, Carol, who lives in the Midwest. When I told her I wanted her to come to New Hampshire to meet the candidates with me, she immediately booked a flight from Columbus, Ohio, to Portsmouth.

Campaign Carol

Carol is a 5' 3" blonde, blue-eyed, walking encyclopedia of presidential trivia. She can recite the name and term date, in chronological order, for each of our United States presidents, and their First Ladies. She has toured the White House, and many former presidents' homes. In 1996, she shook hands with President Clinton. "While he was a *sitting* president," she emphasizes. "Who cares if I didn't vote for him? When I saw him at that whistle stop in Arlington, Ohio, I pushed right through the crowed and yelled 'FOUR MORE YEARS!'"

I'd never had the opportunity to shake hands with *any* president, past, current, or yet-to-be. That was about to change.

"We Want Elizabeth, We Want John!"

At 8:30 a.m. on Saturday, January 5th, I picked Carol up at the airport, and by 9 a.m. we were at the Market Square corner for the "Portsmouth Canvass Kickoff" with John and Elizabeth Edwards. While we were waiting for the Edwards campaign bus to arrive, I panned the crowd with my digital camera and eavesdropped on reporters interviewing enthusiastic Edwards supporters. Cars and delivery trucks crept through the crowded intersection, honking their approval, and the sign-toting mob cheered them on. A young black man, bundled against the cold in a leather jacket and wool muffler, clapped his hands and fired up the crowd with chants and cheers. I glanced around, wondering if anyone in the crowd could tell that Carol and I weren't Edwards supporters. Then I caught sight of Carol, who was now waving a JOHN EDWARDS '08 sign and joining in with:

> "1-2-3-4 we love John more and more,
>
> 5-6-7-8 win the White House in '08!"

I shook my head at her.

"What?" Carol laughed. "Hey, we're here for the handshake." Then she elbowed me and whispered, "Look, the cheerleader is taking his jacket off. I bet the bus will be here soon."

Sure enough, off came the leather jacket to reveal a tweed sports coat. The young Edwards aide discarded his megaphone, assumed a dignified demeanor, and spoke quietly into his cell phone. Within seconds, the "Main Street Express" pulled around the corner and directly into the waiting assembly, amidst cheering, clapping, and sign waving.

Carol and I hustled over to the right side of the bus just as Elizabeth Edwards descended. Cameras clicked and cameramen quickly formed a tight semi-circle around the bus door. John appeared on the top step. Instinctively, I reached above the heads in front of me, waved my hand, and shouted "John, John!" His hand caught mine before the mob swallowed him whole.

Carol beamed. "Good job, Jen. You're one up on me already."

We stood a respectable amount of time listening to Edwards talk about his "Two Americas," and got a few more pictures.

"Wow! Look at the time," I whispered to Carol. "We have to be in Hampstead at 10:30 to catch Romney."

"We're outta here," she agreed. We slipped away from the gathering, and hurried back to my car to the fading sounds of:

> "We want Elizabeth, we want John,
> We want them on the White House lawn..."

Meetin' Mitt

One missed exit and a half hour later we found ourselves standing in front of the Bean Towne Coffee House and Café in Hampstead. We were on the outside, looking in, because the café was packed, shoulder to shoulder, with "wanna-meet-Romney" hopefuls.

We positioned ourselves at the front door, confident that we'd be within handshaking range of Mitt, whether he walked in or out of Bean Towne.

"I can't believe this is working out so well," Carol said. "I've only been in New Hampshire two hours, and I'm about to meet the second candidate!"

With that, Romney's campaign bus appeared in the front parking lot, and his entourage of black SUVs slipped quietly to the back lot. Romney entered the café's back door, and he made a few comments before weaving his way through the crowd toward the front door, and us. We hastily grabbed some Romney brochures, and in minutes a weary looking candidate shook hands with Carol, then me, then numerous others. While we had him in our clutches, we presented our brochures for his autograph.

"Mission accomplished!" We high-fived as we headed back to the highway.

Over a late lunch at Peter Christian's Tavern in New London, consulting the "New Hampshire Presidential Watch" weblog that publicized detailed listings of all candidate events and appearances, we plotted our course for the next three days.

That evening, we watched the Democratic debates, and our neighbor, Keith, dropped by to talk to my husband. He chided us when he learned that we intended to meet every candidate. He proceeded to throw out derogatory remarks about several of them, but when he spouted off about Bill Richardson's toupee, Carol felt compelled to speak up.

"What makes you think it's a toupee?" she challenged Keith.

"Just look at it," Keith gestured to the TV, where Richardson sat, deep in debate with Clinton and Obama.

I had to admit that it *did* look like a rug. It seemed too precise, too sleek, too perfect.

"Well, I'm pretty sure it's all his own hair," Carol retorted, and since she's a hairdresser, I gave her the benefit of the doubt. She'd already scrutinized John Edwards' hair at the morning's rally, and determined that he did, indeed, have it colored.

All of this discussion about toupees and hair color must have piqued my daughter's curiosity, because she walked into the kitchen, sat down with us at the table, and announced that she wanted to go to an Obama rally.

"You're in luck," I told her. "We see him tomorrow, right after the Huckabee Chowder Fest."

Carol grabbed our Presidential Watch blogs, and excitedly scanned the pages. "Any way we can work Hillary into tomorrow's schedule, too? Britt, you really should see her, if for nothing other than historical value. After all, she's a United States Senator *and* a former First Lady!"

Britt rolled her eyes. We had her, though. She was buckled in my Chrysler "Presidential Watch Pacifica" the next morning at 0900 sharp.

Yuckin' It Up With Huck and Chuck

At 10:00 a.m., Sunday, January 6th, we pulled into the parking lot of Windham Center School. From all directions, people walked briskly toward the auditorium doors. The risers in front of the stage were already filled; cameramen and onlookers buzzed around behind them. To the left ran three long tables weighed down with massive vats of steaming chowder. Carol hastily grabbed Huckabee buttons and bumper stickers for all three of us, and hurried us over to a left side door near the front of the room.

Throughout the next half hour, we were jostled and pressed ever tighter against other Huckabee supporters who continued to arrive until the auditorium was packed shoulder to shoulder. Somehow we managed to hold our place in the first row behind the barrier rope, and we were at our post when Mike and Janet Huckabee entered the door amidst whoops and hollers. Carol and Britt caught Huckabee's hand first, and when he got to me, I was impressed that he took my hand, shook it firmly, looked me straight in the eye and thanked me for coming.

Huckabee took the stage and delighted the audience with folksy quips. Then another hubbub arose, as Chuck Norris and his wife entered the side door and joined him onstage. With warmth and sincerity, Huck and Chuck held everyone's attention. I was beginning to relax and even started to eye the chowder table when Carol reminded me that we needed to be in Derry soon for the Obama rally. Clutching our Huckabee buttons, we slipped out quietly.

Obama-rama!

Just a short drive, and a few minutes later, we found ourselves at Pinkerton Academy in Derry, and we quickly found the end of a line of people that already stretched from the front door to the end of the building and doubled back the entire length of the parking lot. Here we waited, and waited, and after the doors opened and the line snaked into the building, we waited some more. But it was worth it, because the atmosphere was electric. Risers filled with young and old, black and white; they waved signs proclaiming, "CHANGE WE CAN BELIEVE IN" and "OBAMA '08" and swayed to the music of John Mayer's "Waiting on the World to Change."

People continued to roll in, and we picked up our pace. Carol assessed the scene in the auditorium, and then hustled us over to the left side of the stage. Only the handicapped seating section separated us from the corridor from which Obama would appear. We looked around for Obama signs, but they'd all been snatched up.

When Obama finally took the stage, he dazzled the crowd with personal charm and eloquent speech. He promised change, and encouraged us to hope, but offered few specifics. Carol and I snapped pictures of the candidate, the crowd, and the secret service men. Britt edged ever closer to the semi-circle barricade that curved around the stage, and pulled Carol and me up into the small pockets of space beside her. When Obama left the stage and began making his way around the semi-circle, his secret service men fanned out ahead of him, and advised all of Obama's well-wishers to keep their hands out of their pockets and in plain view. Carol dutifully positioned her petite, freckled hand on the top of the barricade, poised and ready for the handshake. She turned to tell Britt and me to remember to study his face carefully as he went by. "It will all go by in a blur, so be sure to stay focused."

Obama approached, and his hands rose and fell as they rode the rippling sea of arms waving in front of him. When he got to us, all three of us grasped his hand momentarily, and he smiled warmly at our beaming faces. He moved on to three black women beside us. When one of them whispered something to him, he responded by kissing her on the cheek. As Obama disappeared into the crowd, the lady's two companions bobbed up and down and patted her shoulders.

"He kissed you! You got a kiss from Barack!"

The lucky woman put her hand to her face and looked like she'd swoon. Caught in the moment, she didn't even know he'd kissed her. Carol should have talked to her about staying focused.

It was dark when we left Pinkerton Academy, and far too late to make the drive to Hampton for Hillary's "Time to Pick a President" event. We drove back to North

Sutton for supper, and pored over our Presidential Watch pages until we'd found a way to work Hillary into the next day's schedule.

Nice Hair!

We were up at dawn. "No need for breakfast, Carol," I reminded her. "We're meeting Bill Richardson at Dunkin' Donuts." We downloaded our digital cameras and hit the highway.

We took Exit 9 off Route 93 in Manchester, and headed directly to the Dunkin' Donuts on Beech Street. We plopped down at a table with our glazed and maple frosted doughnuts and hot coffee. I looked at Carol. "You know, this is so unlike you."

"What?" Carol grinned.

"We've been on time, or early, for every one of these campaign events. What happened to Hiler time?" Back in Ohio, Hiler time means 15 to 20 minutes later than the scheduled time for any engagement or event.

"Guess it shows you where my priorities lie," Carol laughed.

We looked around. Plenty of empty tables yet. We shouldn't have any trouble cornering Richardson for the handshake here.

We didn't. When he came strolling in the front door, we saw his eyes focused on the doughnut counter. We cut him off at the pass. I shook his hand, and next thing I knew, Carol had him deep in conversation. I only heard snippets.

"...my sister-in-law in Albuquerque just loves you..." I heard her say as she pumped his hand. He looked her in the eye, but I swear I saw Carol's eyes travel, ever so subtly, up to his hairline. I made a mental note. Carol was right. That man had a beautiful head of lustrous black hair, barely any gray, and definitely all his own.

Bill worked the small crowd, laughing and chatting with a group of students, but inching persistently toward the doughnut counter. Hey-who could blame him? He's a big man, and this campaigning surely has to work up an appetite. There probably aren't a lot of Dunkin' Donuts between Santa Fe and Albuquerque, either!

Before leaving, Carol and I each had our pictures taken with Bill and acquired autographed Richardson buttons. As we walked out, we joined in merrily with the sign-toting supporters, chanting:

"B-I-L-L, yes we can, yes we will!"

Campaigning with Baggage

"Where to next?" Carol asked.

"Dover. To see Hillary."

"What time?"

"12:15, at a place called the McConnell Center."

We were there by 10:45.

"Wow—we are good," we congratulated each other as we crossed the parking lot and joined a group waiting on the steps of the building. A sign said the doors opened at 11:00 a.m.

True, we really were getting the hang of this face-to-face, meet-the-candidate mission. So far, we were batting a thousand, and our confidence must have begun to exude, because a woman about our age tapped Carol on the shoulder and said, "I couldn't help but overhear some of your conversation. Have you met some of the other candidates?"

We filled her in on Edwards, Romney, Huckabee, Obama, and Richardson.

"I've never done anything like this before," she admitted. "I live near Boston, and I had a day off, and decided—what the heck—I may never get a chance like this again. I really want to meet Hillary."

"It's easier than you think to get up close and personal. It's all in where you stand," Carol assured her.

"Well, I'm sticking with you. You look like you know what you're doing."

When the doors opened, our new friend, Karen, from Boston, was right on our heels as we sprinted to the front, just right of the stage. While the event jockeys threw free T-shirts into the frenzied audience, we jockeyed to a position in the first row. Carol pointed to a door a few feet to the right of us. "She'll probably come out there," she whispered to Karen.

Seconds later, Hillary emerged, wearing a blue pantsuit and flanked by security personnel. Eyes wide, Hillary beamed at her enthusiastic supporters, and clutched our hands as she strode toward the stage. After a short introduction, Hillary took charge of the event with a few opening remarks. Women holding "HILLARY FOR PRESI-DENT" signs in one hand and cameras in the other leaned over the horseshoe-shaped barricade, faces turned upward, raptly attentive to the candidate's every word.

"I have a vision for America to be the country it should be in the 21st century," Hillary announced to the cheering onlookers. She leaned toward the audience, and hammered her point home with outstretched arm. "To rebuild a strong and prosperous middle class…"

"You go, girl!" someone shouted.

"…and to reform this government so it actually works for all Americans again."

Men and women clapped, whistled, and waved their signs. After the hubbub subsided, Hillary criss-crossed the stage, pointing here, then there, inviting and answering one question after another.

As the rally drew to a close, and Hillary began the hand shaking circuit, Carol stepped away from her place at the front, and motioned to a young woman standing behind her.

"Here, you take my place. I shook hands with her when she walked in. Hurry! She's heading this way."

With that, Carol plowed her way to the back of the pack of people clamoring to talk to Hillary. An instant later, Carol was approached by a man toting a huge camera, and an attractive blonde woman with a microphone. The next thing I knew, my buddy Carol was deep in conversation with Christa Delcamp from Boston 7 News. The interview lasted about three minutes. Christa wanted to know what Carol thought of the rally, and how she felt Hillary did during the Q and A. Then came the zinger. What did Carol think about former President Bill Clinton campaigning for and with Hillary?

Carol cocked her head to one side and thought about it. Tilting her hand from side to side, she answered, "Mixed feelings. It's like, he's had his turn, and it's her time now. And…he *does* have a little baggage."

Christa concluded the interview, her cameraman motioned to his wristwatch, and the pair hurriedly left the auditorium. Karen and I stood, jaws dropped.

"Oh my gosh! Were you nervous?"

"You two talked a long time."

"Do you think it will air?"

We left the McConnell Center, chattering like school girls. Carol stooped to scoop up a "CLINTON COUNTRY" sign on our way out. We said goodbye to Karen in the parking lot.

"So, you secured the Hillary handshake," we said, smiling at her.

"And I got this autographed campaign sign, and a picture of her on my cell phone," Karen added.

"Not bad for your first political rally," we congratulated her.

When we were in the car, I called my son. "Matt, oh, I'm so glad I caught you! You've got to do something for us. Set the DVR to record all of the Channel 7 news events from 4 p.m. on. Carol was interviewed! What's that? Yep, we're having a great time. We're on our way to Exeter to meet John McCain."

"Mac is Back!"

When we reached Exeter, we took a pit stop at a tidy downtown deli for soup and a sandwich. Our pulses quickened as people hurriedly passed the windows and headed toward Town Hall. We gulped the last of our coffee and hustled after them.

It was only 4:30, but darkness was already falling, and a sliver of moon hung low over the cupola of Exeter's Town Hall. Horns honked as a stream of cars jammed the traffic circle. An immense flagpole towered over the gathering of people near the Town Hall front steps. Campaign signs waved, and the jaunty stars and stripes, reigning supreme in their spotlight, waved back.

With the confidence of seasoned candidate stalkers, we elbowed our way to a position up front and center. We were pleased to find ourselves standing abreast of a young couple with a baby in a stroller.

"The candidates still stop and kiss babies, don't they?" I asked Carol.

A tide of humanity welled up behind us and pushed us closer and closer to the steps and to the legion of school children standing there holding signs that said "IRISH FOR McCAIN." The crowd control aides tried, unsuccessfully, to reserve a narrow exit trail for the McCain entourage.

Carol and I chatted with the young couple while we waited for the "Straight Talk Express" bus to swing by with McCain. They were from Haverhill, MA, and as a teacher, she wasn't happy with what Romney did with education when he was Governor. They felt Richardson was qualified but, sadly, didn't have a chance. We mentioned that Obama was more eloquent than Hillary, but Hillary injected more specifics into her speech, and was open to questions.

"Well—that's a new technique that she put into action, just today," the man informed us. "Obama's been narrowing the gap on her in the polls."

"McCain's our only option," his wife interjected. "That's why we're here, at night, with a baby," she laughed.

Where was John, anyway? One of the cheerleading aides appeared on the front steps, and soon he had the whole crowd chanting, "Mac is back, Mac is back!" Signs waved. Hands clapped. The baby wailed.

"C'mon, John," Carol whispered through clenched teeth.

All eyes turned to the front door of Exeter Town Hall, as John and Cindy McCain finally stepped out in the spotlight focused on the front steps. McCain greeted the appreciative, sign-waving crowd warmly, and delivered an impassioned speech. He closed with, "My friends, I'll get Bin Laden if I have to follow him to the gates of Hell!"

Cheers erupted, and then John and Cindy descended the front steps and began to make their way through the crowd. Carol and I were among the first to greet McCain and shake his hand. I had him sign an "IRISH FOR McCAIN" poster that I'd acquired moments before he'd appeared. Carol, whose son was in the Army, thanked McCain for supporting the military. McCain put his hand on her shoulder. "God bless you," he said.

Beneath the waving American flag and a clear night sky, the McCains zigzagged through their sea of supporters. John appeared to have all the time in the world, as he paused to exchange a few words with everyone who greeted him. At the end of the gauntlet, the "Straight Talk Express" waited to speed the candidate and his wife away to their next engagement.

Carol and I had one more engagement ourselves before we called it a night. My husband caught me on my cell phone, and asked if we were at a Romney event.

"Not yet," I answered, "but we're thinking about dropping in on the 'Ask Mitt Anything' Town Hall meeting in Bedford on our way home, since we didn't get to hear him talk at the Bean Towne Café."

"I just wondered," he said, "because Carl Cameron is on TV right now at a Romney thing, and I wondered if I should look for you in the crowd."

I turned to Carol. "Carl Cameron's at the Romney event in Bedford."

Carol had already shaken hands with Romney on Saturday, so she wasn't sure if she needed to see him again. But when I told her that Carl was within reach, she exclaimed, "How soon can we be there?!"

Campaign Carl

In less than 45 minutes, we'd located Bedford's McKelvie Middle School. Cars filled the lot, and lined the roads in every direction. We walked nearly a half mile and slipped in a back door of the school. A mass of others waited outside of the auditorium. Crowd control officers allowed one person in for every person who exited, so as the people trickled in and out, Carol and I pressed ever closer to the door.

Romney had the supporters inside the packed room eating out of his hand as he delivered an inspirational speech about better education and stricter immigration laws. The audience applauded and cheered. The onlookers craned their necks. When the Q & A began, a bevy of cameramen made their way out, and an elderly lady and I slipped in, unnoticed. I looked back. No Carol. Uh-oh, that was bad, because directly in my sights stood Carl Cameron. I photographed him surreptitiously. It seemed he was packing his gear. I walked over, introduced myself, and told him that my friend was just dying to meet him. I motioned over toward Carol. She was still held at bay by the crowd police. Carl looked over and smiled. A few more people left, and like a thoroughbred charging out of the gates, Carol rushed forward.

"Carl Cameron! Campaign Carl! I wanted to meet you even more than I wanted to meet Romney!"

He seemed pleased, amused, and a bit surprised at all of the attention. A campaign aid sitting nearby offered to photograph us with Carl, and Carol and I eagerly handed our cameras to her. After the photo, Carl told us that he was leaving soon to drive up to Dixville Notch, to cover the historical casting of the first New Hampshire primary votes at The Balsams Grand Resort.

Carol and I left, exhilarated, but thankful that we were done with our campaign coverage for the night. An hour later, we were home, and my family was eager to hear about our experiences. The first order of business was fast-forwarding through three recordings of Boston 7 News. Britt operated the remote, my husband, Ron, observed from the recliner, and Carol and I stood watching expectantly. Four o' clock... nothing. Five o' clock...nothing. Six o' clock...BINGO! On the television screen, we spotted a red, white, and blue sweater and Carol's smiling face.

"I can't believe it! You're on. You made it!"

Carol and I hugged each other, jumped up and down, and hopped around the living room. It was only a short clip of the original interview, focusing on Carol's views about whether or not Bill Clinton was helpful to Hillary's campaign. In the segment, General Wesley Clark, another woman from the rally, and a big shot in the New Hampshire democratic committee all commented that Bill was a great asset to Hillary. Only Carol offered the opposing view.

Upon analysis, I thought Carol interviewed very well. There was extensive analysis, too. In the next few days, I showed it to my neighbors, my son and his friends who were home from college, the guys who were refinishing the floors…

Goodbye, Rudy Tuesday

We had one more day. Tuesday, January 8th, primary election day, had arrived. This was our last chance to catch Rudy Giuliani, so we headed to an 11:30 a.m. "Meet and Greet" at the Puritan Backroom Restaurant in Manchester. We didn't need to be creative to get a good position at this event. The restaurant was nearly empty when we arrived. Rudy had maintained a low profile in New Hampshire during the past few days. Rumor was that he was saving his money and effort for the big winner-take-all Florida primary. When Rudy barreled through the door of the Puritan Backroom, there were more cameramen than supporters there to see him.

Carol and I shook hands with the former New York City Mayor within seconds after he arrived. His communications assistant whisked him over to the designated press area where he took part in a regimented interview and photograph session. It was disrupted by the grand entrance of another presidential candidate, known as Vermin Supreme.

Everyone's attention turned to a man wearing a tattered work boot on his head, and a golden cloak adorned with a spider web design. He looked a little like Fidel Castro with his scruffy beard and piercing eyes. He paraded around the restaurant and shouted insults at Rudy.

Clearly loving the sensation he created, Vermin fielded questions from the press while cameras flashed and clicked. When two little girls passed him, he patted their heads and promised them that when he became president, he'd change the legal voting age to five.

"Who is this guy?" some people murmured. "Is he a clown? A kook?"

We later learned that he was a legitimately registered candidate on the Republican ballot, and therefore could not be ejected from the restaurant as a heckler.

As Giuliani prepared to leave, Vermin Supreme created a scene, jumping over chairs in an attempt to get in his face. "Yeah, that's the way, Rudy. In a hurry to get outta here? Well…bye bye, Rudy!" Vermin shouted. "I'll give you a New York minute!"

Rudy beat a hasty retreat to a waiting SUV, as his communications assistant grimly looked on.

The Final Curtain

I once heard a political commentator compare the presidential campaign to one long, drawn-out audition. We try to decide who will best play the part of president, but we never really know if they've been correctly cast until they've had some time in the role. Carol and I enjoyed watching one small portion of the audition, the exits and entrances, the many lines, filled with promises, that each candidate recites on their journey toward winning the Presidency.

At the end of the performance, Carol and I liked all of them. We saw them as ordinary people, as fellow American citizens. People who serve their country in government and the military, who run businesses, raise children, play the guitar, eat doughnuts, offer change, and change their minds. People who get up every day, put on comfortable shoes, and hit the campaign trail so they can meet us and win our votes.

"Eight candidates in four days," Carol sighed, as I drove her to the airport on Tuesday afternoon. "It's all so exciting here. I could never have done this back home."

How true. For meeting your presidential candidates, there's no place like the intimate political theatre of New Hampshire. Their stage may be a school gymnasium, a café, the steps of Town Hall, or a doughnut shop. Whatever the venue, it is always local, personal, and accessible, allowing their audience to walk right up onstage with them, shake their hand, and look them in the eye.

"It's been a great show," Carol winked, "but you'd better keep moving so you don't miss the last curtain call."

"What do you mean?" I asked.

"I mean," Carol laughed, "you'd better hurry back home, get behind that curtain, and VOTE!"

IN THE HEAT OF BATTLE

It hadn't rained since early May. At least no real rain to speak of. Once or twice, a brief sprinkling shower rolled by, depositing a few meager drops of moisture, as if God was wringing out a giant dishcloth. The dirty drops plopped on the dusty ground, and evaporated before they could soak in.

It was our fifth summer on the little farm. This was our first home, complete with an old white farmhouse, a weathered red bank barn, and four acres of lawn and meadow surrounded by our neighboring farmers' fertile fields and woodlands. Each summer, we watched the waving green velvet cornstalks, with their butter-yellow tassels, gradually turn to rustling amber and then to October's bountiful harvest of gold.

That spring, we cheered the local farmers on, happy to see the planting season progress smoothly. Corn in by late April, beans in by early May. We waited and worried with our neighbors as June dragged by without any rain, and watched helplessly as the young green sprouts slowly, agonizingly, shriveled and browned in the merciless summer heat.

Despite our concern over the drought, we carried on with our summer activities as usual. We celebrated July 4th with fireworks and a huge family reunion at our home. When the last station wagon pulled out of our dusty driveway, we breathed a sigh of relief, carried a week's worth of trash to the burn pile beyond the orchard fence, and lit it.

We ambled over to the nearby hammock, and within minutes, my husband and I were dozing off in the cool shade of an immense silver maple. Through the late afternoon lull, I heard an odd crackling sound. I tried to ignore it, but couldn't. Reluctantly leaving the comfortable swing, I walked across the baked lawn toward the barn, and in an instant, I was fully awake.

"Ron," I shrieked, "the field's on fire!"

Startled from his slumber, he leaped out of the hammock and ran to the tool shed. I ran to the house. He emerged from the shed armed with a shovel, and I followed him carrying a broom. We sprinted toward the pasture, and hurtled over the board fence. Frantically, we worked away at the fire, which now encompassed a circular area about twelve feet wide. His shovel was no match for the cracked, hard crust of ground, and as he hacked away at it, the shovel handle splintered and broke off just above the blade. I continued beating the flames until the straw broom caught fire and was reduced to a blackened stump.

The fire was raging now, its blazing orange flares searing our skin. The breeze kicked up and the flames snaked farther out on every side. Burning embers jumped to catch hold of the tips of the wizened meadow grass. Eyes burning, choking on smoke, we paused. Ron was fully focused on the fire in front of him, but I envisioned an inferno sweeping up the hill and engulfing our barn before marching onward through the parched cornfields to devour half the township.

We cast our useless tools aside. Ron shouted to me to run for the garden hose, but I was already on my way. An alarmed neighbor met me at the corner of our barn.

"Do you want me to call the fire department?" he yelled.

"Yes," I croaked.

With legs of rubber, I stumbled to the house and attached a length of hose to the outside spigot. Fully uncoiled, it reached only to the edge of the driveway. I needed at least three more lengths. I sprinted up the barn hill, tripped and fell, sliding in the dust and grit. I clawed at several coils of garden hose lying on the barn floor, tugging and pulling them down the hill to the extended piece lying nearby. I tried to focus on the task, but one look at the fiery field sent me on a new wave of despair, fearful of the flames reaching the far fence and the woods beyond. In my mind, I saw a charred stand of twisted timber smoldering on the horizon.

I struggled to attach the lengths of hose. Still not enough! Back to the house I ran, and spun the spigot to the full ON position, then raced to the tool shed for buckets. I now fully understood the term "cotton-mouth" as I gagged on the dryness.

The cistern water level was low from the drought, and when I plunked the nozzle into the bucket, a mere trickle rolled out. My head began to spin; my knees buckled. The fire department was our only hope now. Where were they?!

The sound of an engine cut through my fog of panic. Were they here? Through the haze of smoke over the meadow, I saw something circling round and round the flames. What was it? Who was it? It looked familiar. Ah, my hero! My knight in shining armor, atop his noble steed?

No, just my husband aboard a used, twelve horsepower Snapper lawnmower, that devoured the fire's food like a hungry orange monster. I watched in awe and admiration as he mowed three swaths of tall grass around the fire's circumference.

As the fire burned itself out inside its charred circle, Ron and I kept watch at the edge to extinguish any stray embers. With our meager water supply, we doused the last of the burning patches, and fell to the ground, exhausted, but relieved.

A second later we heard sirens---way off in the distance at first—then ever nearer, coming from every direction. Two pick-up trucks wheeled into our driveway, throwing gravel. Across the eastern field, we saw a trail of billowing dust, and another truck appeared. It bounced over the cracked earth, snapping off scraggly cornstalks and shredding them in its grille. The truck shuddered to a stop beside the meadow gate. Doors flew open and men scrambled out, hiking up overall straps and pulling on knee-high rubber boots. The Liberty Township volunteer fire department had arrived!

As we proudly explained that we'd managed to extinguish the fire all by ourselves, the glint of anticipation in their eyes vanished. The eager warriors had marched to the battlefield only to find that the enemy had already surrendered. With stooped shoulders, they slipped off their overalls and piled back into their trucks.

"Any idea how the fire got started?" asked the fire chief.

Ron just stood there.

Puzzled, I looked at him, and then blurted, "Well, yeah, it was from our burn pile. A spark must have gone airborne and caught on the tall grass."

Too late, I realized my mistake, and we stood there, sheepishly, waiting for him to levy a fine on us. He scratched his head, lectured us about the risks of burning during a severe drought, and wearily reviewed burning permit rules and regulations. He climbed into his truck, nodded, and drove away.

~ ~ ~

Quite a few years have passed since that stifling July day. We've endured many rainy spells as well as droughts, and learned some of life's hard lessons through experience.

A wise old farmer once told me...

"Never seen it so dry that it didn't get wet again,
never seen it so wet that it didn't get dry again."

I like to view the weather, and life, with that saying in mind.

THE CHIEF

It's a good thing we didn't have "Cash for Clunkers" when I was a teenager, or I'd never have driven the best car of my life. It was a 1969 Pontiac Catalina station wagon, with a 400 V8 engine, 97,000 miles. It had some rust spots on the outside and some torn vinyl on the inside, and someone had to hold the tailgate window steady when it was raised or lowered. My dad presented it to me soon after I got my driver's license. It was lowest on the totem pole of drivable machines among the fleet of used vehicles on our farm. Dad didn't need it anymore, and he knew that it was heavy and dependable. It was a safe ride for his daughter.

I didn't care that my first car was big, clunky and turquoise, as long as it got me to school, to work, and to the drive-in movies with a gang of giggling girlfriends. We pushed the safety belts into the crevice where seat and seat back met, so that we could easily slide passengers in and out. Four in the front seat, four or five in the back seat, and at least three in the tailgate-accessed rear seat.

I loved cruising around town in this tank; I loved the boat-like steering wheel, cool and slick in my hands. I loved the Chief Pontiac decorative emblem, and the little silhouette of the Chief that lit up red when I was low on gas, which was often. I didn't care that it was a gas guzzler, because gasoline didn't cost much then; two dollars' worth kept me going all week.

One summer Saturday, as my friends piled in for our day's adventure, my visiting uncle surveyed our spacious conveyance, then whistled, rolled his eyes, and said, "Don't bring any ugly boys home." All of the relatives waved goodbye as the teenage-laden Catalina slowly crunch-crunched its way down our long gravel driveway.

After our day-long outing, I dropped all of my girlfriends at their respective houses, and headed home. A fiery August sun had begun its leisurely descent as I breezed west on Highway 40. All the windows were down. The radio blared an *Eagles* hit. "Put me on a highway, show me a sign, and take it to the limit, one more time…" I sang at the top of my lungs, my long brown hair swirling around my head, the sticky summer sweat drying to salt on my skin.

I may have been driving a little too fast, and I realized a little too late that it was time to make a left turn off of the freeway and onto my country road. I started to glide into the left lane but an old rattletrap blocked my way. My cruisin' Catalina was in no mood to slow down and wait its turn behind this heap, so I stepped on it, sped past it in the right lane, then whipped into the left lane just a few feet ahead of the truck's jiggling bumper. A few yards ahead was my road, so I hit the brakes and prepared to negotiate my turn.

Don't mess with an old drunk in a '57 Chevy pick-up! He careened into the right lane, stomped on it, and in a split second our clunkers were abreast. Through his open window he shouted curses and shook his hairy arm at me.

"Yeah, I cut you off, you old geezer. So what?" I thought to myself. I turned onto my road. To my horror, he slammed on his brakes, made a quick U-turn, then yanked a right that put him on my tail. He was still screaming and shaking his fist. I was half afraid he would hurl a beer can through my open tailgate window.

I tromped on the accelerator and the chase was on. My house was about a mile up the road. I'd gotten a pretty good glimpse of this lunatic back at the turn. With his tattered flannel shirt and faded ball cap, three-day-old stubble and bloodshot eyes, he definitely qualified as an "ugly boy" and no way was I going to bring him home! So I floored it and zoomed past my driveway, my heart pounding, my palms slick with sweat.

We were heading south, bumper to bumper. The road made a 90-degree turn to the left, and I gained a little on him just before this bend. He skidded into the sharp turn, and I saw a cloud of dust in my rearview mirror. When it cleared, there he was, still close behind me, his truck jerking from side to side as we raced over the bumpy road. I plunged down the hill and over the bridge, my tires rat-tatting on the wood planks. 50, 60, 70 miles per hour my speedometer climbed, and still I saw the blur of faded red behind me, but the gap was widening. Another sharp left just before the school and I grew confident. "I'll take you on this chase all day, Grandpa," I hissed through clenched teeth, "I know these roads like the back of my hand."

As we headed north now, my raging pursuer soon became a distant speck, as old Chief Pontiac hit his stride, gliding from one willy-bump to the next, with the ease and comfort of a yacht on a gently rolling sea. Now I was back at Route 40, with no trace of the madcap maniac in my mirrors. I turned left onto the highway, took a deep breath, patted the dashboard, and calmly steered my faithful station wagon home.

A couple of years later, I went away to college, and the old Chief went away to the scrap yard. But, after all these years, I still have fond memories of my gas guzzling clunker that transported me to independence on the highway of life, and always got me safely home again. Of all the firsts of our youth, first dance, first kiss, first job…there is none quite as memorable as that first taste of freedom that comes with the first car.

THE BINKY FAIRY

My husband and I dutifully read the childhood development manuals and magazines while we prepared for the arrival of our first baby. But we learned that there's nothing like the real thing to wake you up to the realities of parenting. Less than a year into the journey, we hit a bump in the road, caused by that pesky little tool called the pacifier.

~ ~ ~

"Can't you do something?" my husband groaned. "Is he hungry?"

I pushed the crumpled ball of pillow off my ear and glared at him.

"No, he's not hungry," I snapped. "Why don't YOU do something? I have to get up in the morning, same as you."

He mumbled and rolled over, pressed his ear deep into the mattress and pulled the covers over his head.

Muttering, I climbed out of bed…again. I knew what was wrong. It was the damned pacifier. I didn't know how to keep the thing IN his mouth. I'd been up countless times trying.

I tiptoed to our baby's room. At his doorway, I dropped to my hands and knees, and quietly made my way to the base of the crib. Reaching my hand up, around, and through the rails, my contorted fingers bent and twisted until I pinched the pacifier's edge, and ever so carefully guided the rubber nipple back into his mouth. The ear-shattering shrieks subsided, and made way for a rhythmic, suckling sound. Crouched like a cat in the darkness beneath his crib, I waited, heart pounding.

"Yes," I whispered. "Please, God, don't let him spit it out this time."

I imagined being back in my warm cocoon of blankets, feeling slumber envelop me. Maybe I could still catch about three hours of sleep.

I listened.

Gurgling sounds. I squeezed my eyes shut. I crossed my fingers.

"Whaa-a-a-a…"

I jumped to my feet and glowered at him. Startled, his eyes opened wide.

"That's it!" I hissed.

Tucking him in the crook of my left arm, I grabbed the pacifier with my right. His eyes moved from me to the pacifier. For one blessed moment, silence reigned. I pulled the plastic demon away, holding it at arm's length, way above his head. Both little arms reached for it, fists kneading the air.

"No, no, NO!" I yelled.

His tiny face scrunched into angry creases. Hot tears bubbled from his eyes. Slowly, I brought the pacifier back toward his face. Mesmerized, his mouth opened and closed, soundlessly, hypnotically. I held it at his eye level, and, walking to the bathroom door, said sternly, but calmly, "You see this? No more! NO MORE!" With that, I hurled the dastardly thing into the trash can beside the toilet. His eyes followed its flight until it landed with a plop. He stared silently. My heart pounded.

Then it started. From deep inside him, an eruption of raw emotion burst forth, drowning out the night, filling the house with heart-rending, gut-wrenching cries punctuated by breath-catching sobs. His head looked like a peachfuzz-covered beet. My heart ached for him, but there was no turning back now.

I jiggled him from side to side and patted his bottom as we made our way back to his crib. I cooed. I sang. I rocked. My husband shuffled in. He cradled him in his arms and crooned to him. It was no use. We put him in the crib to cry himself to sleep.

We went back to bed and lay there, overcome with self-loathing and parental guilt.

The crying stopped just before 6 a.m. The alarm clock went off five minutes later.

The next night, he slept straight through.

~ ~ ~

Sixteen years later…

I picked my daughter up from a sleep over at her friend's house.

"How'd it go, honey?" I asked, as she hopped into the car.

"Great! Mom, Paige's little brother is SO cute! They've been trying to wean him off his binky, so they had a ceremony for it last night."

Intrigued, I asked for details.

"Well, for a while now, they've been telling him that someday he'll have to give his pacifier to the 'Binky Fairy'. So, they took him shopping yesterday and got him balloons and a little glittery box. He put his binky in the box, they wrote a note to the fairy on one of the balloons, and they helped him tie the balloons to the box. Then we all went outside and watched it float off into the sky.

"Did he cry?"

"No, first he laughed and clapped. Then he waved until it was out of sight.

I shook my head. "The Binky Fairy, huh? No one ever told me about her."

~ ~ ~

Sometimes, moms just have to chuck all of the parenting literature and shoot from the hip, especially when they're sleep deprived. I severed my son's relationship with the pacifier long before we needed the Binky Fairy. Still, it's too bad I didn't meet her a few years ago. Maybe I'll save her for the grandchildren.

Jenny's stories have been published in *Kearsarge Magazine*, and *NH Magazine*. Her favorite authors are David McCullough, Margaret Mitchell, O. Henry, Anna Quindlen, and Mark Twain.

Invitation to Play

The Prompt:

Inspired by the book, The World's Shortest Stories, *our writing group held a contest to write a short story in exactly 55 words (title not included). Jenny won the contest with this submission:*

Old Friends

They placed eight chairs on the beach.

"Six gone."

"Just us now."

"What's your prognosis?" Sadie asked.

"Not good," Julie sighed.

"I can't come here alone next year, Jules."

"So you're ready?"

"If you are."

Julie stirred the powder into their martinis.

"One for the road!"

"To us."

They clinked glasses and watched the sunset.

The Prompt:

In a short exercise designed to help develop character emotions, writers were challenged to write a dialogue between themselves and an emotion that they chose at random. Jenny picked the emotion, Anxiety. They began with the line: "My computer screen tells it all..." Here is her exchange (unedited):

Anxiety

"My computer screen tells it all. I have accidentally hit *Reply All* and sent an e-mail to someone not intended to see it."

"Does that make you nervous?"

"Yes."

"Why?"

"Because I've just told my neighbor, and probably now former best friend, that Kara's recipe for lemon bars is much better than hers."

"Wow, she's going to be devastated by that news."

"Hold on, now. Devastated is a strong word."

"How about *crushed?*"

"Whew, that's harsh, too. She's pretty easy going. Maybe she'll laugh it off."

"Or maybe not. What's going on in her life lately?"

"Well, she's under a little stress with her new job."

"Oh yeah, you mean that new job as hospital cafeteria supervisor?"

"Yep, she just started last week, and is still learning the ropes, but she'll soon have it under control."

"Whoa there. Think of that! When word gets out that your friend Kara makes a much better lemon bar than the new cafeteria supervisor, she'll be embarrassed, annoyed, maybe even demoted."

"Oh, stop, stop, STOP! She's been so busy with the new job that she probably hasn't checked her e-mail yet anyway."

"That little note about how much creamier and sweeter Kara's lemon bars are than hers will be sitting in her *Inbox* just waiting for her."

"Creamier and sweeter? Did I say that in the note?"

"Uh-huh, you did. You also said Terri's lemon bars tasted a little sour."

"Oh, no, did I? Are you sure? Did I say sour!? She'll be…"

"Devastated?"

"Yes! Maybe even worse…"

"Crushed?"

"Yes, YES, crushed, too. Oh, I can't believe I said all of that. I'm looking back at that note. I don't believe you."

"Go ahead. Look away. There it is. Your computer screen tells it all."

The Prompt:

I collect words, phrases, and images to use for prompts. For one class, I cut out headlines and phrases from magazines and asked the writers to randomly draw seven slips of paper. They were to arrange them in an order that felt right (once the order is set, do not change it). Write a story using the phrases as chapter headings (15 minutes). Here is Jenny's story that she entitled Freedom:

Freedom

A Fast Getaway...

I'd thought about leaving for quite a long time. She was controlling, manipulative, demanding. I was no longer in charge of my life--MY LIFE! That's the problem. It's my life, not hers! I had to make a break for it, so I planned my escape.

Dawn of a New Day...

It started out like any other day. Up at seven, a quick jaunt outdoors, breakfast. Usually a nap after that. But today, according to plan, I faked a need to go outdoors again. So unlike me, but if I acted agitated I knew that she'd be puzzled, but would let me have my freedom...and, sure enough, it worked. She opened the screen door and out I trotted. The sun was popping up over the trees east of the driveway. I put my nose way up in the air...sniffed, turned my body to the west, and began running.

The Perfect Coat...

I ran and ran. I heard her calling, fuming mad now. I never looked back. Neighbors were already out walking. I had to avoid them. I veered off the road and into the wooded area on the fringe of the lake. Brambles caught in my coat, but they never slowed me down 'cause I was made for this terrain. It was warming up already. I could feel the heat rising from the moist ground. No problem. I was almost to the lake, and, once there, I'd jump in and swim around as long as I felt like it. My fluffy coat would buoy me and I'd relax and relish every moment of my new-found freedom.

Will Somebody Please Explain...

But wait a minute! Is that her, right there at the edge of the lake, jumping out of her Pacifica, leash in hand? How did she find me already? Does she really think I'm going to swim back to her, tail between my legs, and give up just like that?

Moving On...

I paddled to the left and headed to the inlet, my tail steering me deftly, like a giant rudder. A few more strokes and I'd disappear amongst the reeds. Maybe I'd hang out for the afternoon behind a beaver lodge, well out of sight.

Stop Dreaming...

It sounded like a plan, but it didn't take long for reality to set in. My feet soon touched the mucky bottom, and I couldn't find firm footing. I slogged through squishy mud. Dead slimy leaves caught in my fur and bogged me down. My heart was pumping. My tongue was hanging out of my mouth. Duck poop was getting in my eyes. Wow…this freedom thing isn't what I'd hoped it would be. It seemed like a great idea yesterday, but now the dream wasn't so enticing.

What Makes or Breaks You...

I'm tired. I'm hot. But most of all, I'm hungry. Guess I never thought about that. Suddenly, the thought of my big plastic bowl, full of kibbles, consumed me. The heck with freedom! I want lunch!!

THESAURUS ENTRY: compassion
PART OF SPEECH: *noun*
DEFINITION: tender feeling
SYNONYMS: benevolence, grace, charity, empathy, heart, mercy, kindness, softheartedness

Susan Joy Bellavance

WORD WEAVES AND TAPESTRIES

I am a seeker. My passion is for truth, beauty, goodness, and faith. My desire is to wrap words around hearts to make them feel uplifted and encouraged. I love the dignity and nobility of the human spirit and am inspired to capture it with ink and paper, the way artists do with oils and canvas. My mind is filled with words to bursting, but mostly the cork gets stuck and nothing comes out. I do a lot of staring at white sheets of paper. Without the help of family and friends, I would never have undertaken this mysterious journey of words and awakenings.

My husband, Dale, is the president of the "You Can Do It" committee, co-chairing with my daughter Sophia (20), an English/Writing major at Franciscan University in Steubenville, Ohio. My fan club, Marguerite (15), my younger daughter, is a high school sophomore at Trivium School in Lancaster, Massachusetts. We reside in

Newbury, New Hampshire, but I am originally from the Annapolis, Maryland, area. I come from a large, brawling Sicilian family; that is probably why I never run out of colorful ideas.

Besides greenhouse management, and teaching junior high, my wildest, most creative job was implementing a horticulture therapy program for an institution in Crownsville, Maryland.

I began writing poetry when I was about 13, and poetry was all I wrote until about three years ago, when I stepped into the *Words in Play* workshops. Writing with the support of a writers' group opens up a vista of possibilities that I would not accomplish on my own—I have begun writing short stories, magazine articles, children's stories, and novels. My dream is to finish the several lengthy pieces in which I am immersed. I am sure my writing group will keep me corralled until they are completed. Thank God for that.

Deb's Insights:

From the moment I met Susan, I was enthralled with her ability to think in metaphor. This might be related to her deep faith. It could also be related to the many layers of Susan; on the surface she is a loving wife and mother raising two children in a sleepy town in central New Hampshire. When you learn that Susan lived for years amidst abject poverty in the slums of Harlem and Rome as a novitiate in Mother Teresa's order, you begin to understand that this person has experienced life in ways few people ever know. That experience informs her writing on many levels.

Susan is fierce and funny, tender and joyful, realistic and silly, a poet and a chronicler. As a writer, Susan is first and foremost a storyteller. She has dozens of stories clamoring inside her head; they play like movies in her mind. She amazes the writing group with her feedback on the work of others; her ability to see the interconnectedness of a piece is astounding.

Susan is also a word crafter; when she needs a word that does not exist, she makes one up. (My personal favorite is *krinky*: the snack you eat with your mid-day cup of coffee.) She's in good company; William Shakespeare coined about 1700 new words during his career. It's a marvelous talent.

Susan is now pitching her stories at publishers' conferences; she has completed a children's chapter book and is well into two other novels. She writes articles and poetry to fill in the gaps.

SISTER LUCY AND THE PAYBACK

The news spread like wildfire: Pope John Paul II was arriving in New York on October 2, 1979. There was an outpouring of excitement at our convent in the South Bronx, where I was a 23-year-old postulant, a newcomer learning about religious life. The electric excitement increased wattage when Sister Priscilla, the Superior of the house of the Missionaries of Charity, announced that she would be getting passes for all of us to go to the papal Mass, as well as some of the other events connected to the Holy Father's visit. I kept thinking, "Wow, the Pope, coming here..." It took awhile for it to sink in.

Before papal sojourning became a commonplace event, the average Catholic in America knew that they had a threefold chance of a papal encounter: slim, fat, and none. That is, unless you were a diplomat, or rich enough to travel to Europe, or...if the Pope decided to come and see *you* instead. John Paul II was an intriguing person—a ruddy, vigorous, Polish pope with a mischievous smile and a captivating heart that reached out to everyone. I was ecstatic to have this chance.

The house was full with 20 or so high-spirited, beaming sisters. Some were newly arrived aspirants, some postulants who had been there for almost a year, and the rest were professed sisters, those who had taken vows after five years' preparation. All were going about their daily duties with a lift in their step; it would take an act of God to change the schedule of the Missionaries of Charity. Business as usual was our daily bread: visits to the shut-ins; serving at the soup kitchen; hospital visits; the household chores—all set to the beat of a prayer life that strung the common events of the day together like a rosary. Tomorrow would be different. *He* was coming to New York and *we* had passes!

That evening, after a dinner of soup, bread, and supercharged conversation so loud that we could hardly hear the bell ring, we dispersed to perform our after dinner chores, and prepare for recreation and evening prayer. (Recreation meant sitting on the floor and sewing the holes in our saris while making each other laugh with the funny stories of the day.) After a meal, you simply picked up your bowl and flatware, washed it in the nearest sink, and put it back on the shelf in the refectory, a fancy name for a room with a picnic table in it. On my way to rinse my dinner dish, I was contemplating how well I had put into effect the latest correction I had been given—not telling jokes while Sister Lydia was eating spaghetti (because it made her choke). Comic timing now included watching to see if Sister Lydia was chewing or not, before the punch line was delivered.

The internal review would have to wait; on my way down to the basement kitchen, I suddenly came upon Sister Lucy, weeping in the corner of the stairway landing. "What is it, Sister?" I said, as keeping the silence wasn't compatible with charity at the moment. Her tear-stained face was bent downward. I couldn't imagine what had happened to her—she had just been laughing with the rest of us in the refectory only moments ago.

Sister Lucy was all sweetness. A Quebec native with an endearing French accent, she was a slight, pale creature with bachelor-button-blue eyes, and the propensity to drop, spill, or break whatever she had in her hands. To our group, she was pure delight, a gentle, sensitive soul of childlike purity and goodness.

"Sister Priscilla needs me to stay home tomorrow evening to care for her, and to make her supper while everyone else goes to see the Holy Father," Sister Lucy explained through her tears. She continued to weep, lifting her tiny gold-rimmed glasses from her eyes to wipe her tears. I thought for a moment that I understood the problem.

"Oh, Sister, I'm sorry. That is going to be so hard. To be stuck here when everyone else is going. You won't get to see the Holy Father."

"That is not the problem. That is not why I am crying," she said. "I have to cook for Sister Priscilla." She stopped and looked at me to see if I comprehended her plight.

"So?"

"I can't do that. I will make mistakes and she will be cross with me." The tears were renewed.

I had forgotten how terrified Lucy was of our superior. Although she looked hale and vigorous, Sister Priscilla had wracked her body caring for the poor, the lepers, and the dying in India. She was a tall, regal woman with beautiful Indian skin and large dove eyes. Her British accent gave her charm, as well as an air of authority. Sister Priscilla had an indomitable character. She was all order, justice, intense love, and surprisingly, a lot of humor, with an emphasis on storytelling and practical jokes. Now, after so many years of service, it was Sister Priscilla herself who needed some assistance when she had a bad day. Although she rarely mentioned her pains, her eyes revealed a different story. Her knees were inflamed and arthritic; she had difficulty swallowing, and she suffered other internal ailments. Despite her infirmities, she was a formidable woman on a mission. Remarkably unstoppable, she was a kind of spiritual typhoon in a blue par sari. It was this side of her that gave Sister Lucy the willies.

The more nervous Sister Lucy got, the more she bumbled. The more she bumbled, the more she frustrated the superior. It was a comical cycle of events for us, but not so funny for Lucy.

I looked at her now, crying like a child, and I could not hold back the words that came out of my mouth, although I couldn't believe I was saying them. It was almost against my will. "Go ask Sister Ancy if I could take your place, and I will stay here and prepare Sister's meal and look after her. You go to see the Holy Father."

"Really? You would do that for me?" she asked, all red-nosed and puffy-eyed.

"Yes. Now go," I said with a gentle push. Off she went.

"What did I just say?! I want to go. What am I thinking?" I have always had an impetuous streak. Something unplanned is always bursting out of me. Sometimes it works toward my divine account, sometimes against it. My heart was already sinking at the prospect of not going to see John Paul II.

Sister Lucy wasted no time locating Sister Ancy. She returned in a short moment, beaming. "Oh, no," I whispered.

"Sister said you could stay home and that I could go in your place," she announced. Then she looked at my face intently. "Are you sure you want to do that?"

No Pope. I lost my chance to see the Pope. *I lost my chance.*

"Of course, I am sure," I said in my most heroic tone. "I wouldn't have asked you if I wasn't sure. You go tomorrow. I will be fine here. You just go..." Off Sister Lucy went, with a light heart and a bright face.

I just stood there withering inside like a plucked dandelion, all perky and sunshiney one moment, and all droopy the next. But I didn't let Sister Lucy see me droop.

The day of the Holy Father's arrival came. All of New York was bustling with excitement and expectation. The visit would be a smash hit even for a celebrity-bored city like New York, the toughest crowd in the world.

Early that afternoon, everyone but me put on her "third set." Each nun in a Missionary of Charity convent has three sets of clothes. One to wear, one to wash in the bucket and hang on the line, and a "third set," a dress set that is saved for special occasions. The third set is wrapped up in cloth and packed away until needed for, let's say, an outing, or A PAPAL VISIT. Every garment was gleaming white, without patches or darning spots.

Everyone's clothing was different. Your dress indicated your level of formation. An aspirant wore a navy skirt and a white blouse for the first six months. The first-year sisters, the postulants, wore all white—white blouse, white ankle-length drawstring skirt, and a white sari, held in place by a piece of rope wrapped around the waist and the corner piece pinned at the shoulder with a cross. The professed sisters, the ones who had taken vows to be sisters, wore the "blue par," a white sari bordered by the three royal-blue stripes over a full-length white cassock, the habit worn by Mother Teresa.

The community gathered in the front hall for instructions from Sister Priscilla, partnered up, and left the house. It looked as if someone had opened a birdcage and released a flock doves. I stood there like a lonely teacher on the last day of school. Everyone gone. Silence. I walked into the chapel.

"Lord, this is killing me. I give this pain to you."

The achy heart refused to leave. I puttered about. I made Sister's dinner. She didn't like the way I made it. I must admit, the eggs were runny and unappealing. Time meandered until it was night. Eventually, the door opened. The flock had returned.

We gathered in the downstairs refectory of the professed sisters. There were stories and accounts, laughter, and a general swelling of hearts, expressing how incredible it had felt to see the Holy Father. As the chatter continued, I put on my best face, but I felt a keen sorrow to have missed it all. Sister Lucy gave me a tender smile. She knew my sacrifice. I'm sure she prayed for me.

~ ~ ~

One year later.

Our group left New York City for Rome, Italy, to prepare to enter the novitiate, a two-year intensive preparation for first vows as Missionaries of Charity. At that time, American groups were sent to Tor Fiscale, a poor suburb of Rome on the outskirts of the city. We studied, prayed, learned to speak Italian, visited the poor, served in the soup kitchen, worked at the men's shelter, and visited hospitals, all in view of discerning our vocation; each novice would decide if she wanted to make this her life or not.

When we first arrived, we met up with our group sisters who would be professed with us in two years, sisters from all over Europe and India. For the first few weeks we stayed in San Gregorio, the home of St. Gregory the Great, where there was a large men's shelter and soup kitchen. The convent was located in what used to be St. Gregory's chicken coop. (Thankfully, it had been remodeled a bit.) There was something deeply satisfying about living in St. Gregory the Great's chicken coop. Not something any of my friends had ever done. In a few weeks, we would go to Tor Fiscale, where there were already 40 other sisters in various stages of formation.

Then some great news: Mother Teresa, who had won the Nobel Peace Prize almost a year before, was on her way to Oslo, Norway. She would spend a few days with us at San Gregorio, before and after receiving the honor. Then she would return to Calcutta.

The day Mother Teresa arrived was perfect delight. The diminutive nun was so powerful, and filled with so much joy! Her presence was like a magnet that pulled the heart. She greeted us with her blessing. With folded hands we bent our heads, and she placed her hands on both sides, saying softly, "God bless you." After we all settled down about her in the professed sisters' refectory, she gave us more thrilling news. The Holy Father, apprised of Mother Teresa's schedule, had contacted her and invited her to come to the Vatican for a Mass of Thanksgiving while she was in Rome. The Holy Father would be sending a bus to San Gregorio in the very early morning, and Mother was to fill it with her sisters. Our group had 22 sisters from about 12 countries. It just so happened that there were 22 seats left on the bus, and Mother Teresa wanted to know if our group would like to go with her to see the Holy Father in the morning. I was dumbfounded. Was this really happening to me?

The bus arrived so early, the fading moon was still silvering a dark sky. Mother Teresa stood at the door of the bus, like a hen shooing her chicks along. We loaded the bus in customary silence, each of us bursting with joy underneath a silent exterior. We rambled along empty streets of sleepy Rome, reciting the rosary aloud. Soon, the sunlight began to rim the ancient city buildings. Then the dome of St. Peter's became visible. We turned the corner to see two Swiss Guards in their bright yellow-striped medieval uniforms, one standing on either side of an arched gateway. They opened the gate, and the bus churned through the gears as we entered archway after archway. We were deep inside the Vatican walls. The bus stopped in front of an ornate doorway. The guards opened the doors and led us to a long stairway. Sister Francesca and I happily ended up on either side of Mother Teresa climbing the stairs. The marble stairway was worn thin in the center; it curved to the shape of our feet. I wondered how many saints, kings, and brigands had climbed these ancient steps. Even now, as Mother Teresa went to celebrate the winning of the Nobel Peace Prize with Pope John Paul II, I realized that this was no small piece of history itself.

The top of the stairs opened to a spacious marble hall. This is one of the rooms where the Holy Father meets visitors. Down to the left, we approached his private chapel. Suddenly, there he was, sitting in the center area on a black marble chair before the altar, the special place where he meditates and prays the Psalms before Mass. His white robe, against the black marble chair, was an intense image that burned into my heart.

There were a few pews behind the Holy Father, but these were quickly filled by our sisters. The only space left was on the floor near him. Some of the sisters had to sit there; I was one of those. The white soutane he wore spilled onto the floor around his chair; without his knowing, I held onto it. While he prayed, I prayed with him.

The front chapel wall curved in a U shape. It was ornamented with mosaics of the early Christian martyrs. On the right behind the altar was a favored Italian saint, Santa Lucia. Then I remembered. It was December 13th, the Feast of St. Lucy, the Patron saint of the sister whose place I had taken instead of going to see the Holy Father in New York. *Remarkable.*

We received communion from the Holy Father, and later, after Mass, he visited with us. His greeting to Mother Teresa was beautiful. Mother had explained to us once that she did not allow people to hug or kiss her due to her vow of chastity, and her desire to keep herself for God alone. When people approached her, she bent her head down, folded her hands and bowed in respect as a greeting. But with the Holy Father, she accepted his greeting out of love for who he was. He was so tall and she, so short. He put his arm around her and kissed her on top of the head saying, "My Mother." The Nobel Prize she had won pleased him greatly.

Soon, Mother began to present us to him, one by one. A photographer, standing next to the Holy Father, took pictures as each person met him. A very noticeable long strand of hair had fallen out from under the Holy Father's small, round zuchetto on his head. It made him look a little untidy for photographs. Being an American, I am sensitive to the media making fun of things religious, especially things Catholic. While I waited my turn to meet him, I got angrier and angrier, thinking, "They are taking pictures to put in some magazine to ridicule him." The angst grew in my heart. I didn't know that the Vatican had its own photographer, and that the picture being taken would eventually become a gift to each one of us. How was I supposed to know? Step by step, closer and closer, I grew angrier and angrier. I remember saying to myself, "No one, no one will make fun of my Holy Father while I'm in the room." By the time it was my turn to greet the Pope, my purpose was set. I reached up and fixed his hair.

He jumped back. "What are you doing?"

"Holy Father," I explained, "Your hair is messed up and they're taking your picture!"

"You must be an Italian," he laughed.

I found out later that sometimes the Italians try to take relics off of saintly persons before they are dead. He thought I was trying to get a *very* personal keepsake.

"Oh, no, Holy Father, I'm an American."

He leaned forward, raised his eyebrows knowingly, and insisted, "*Someone* in your family is Italian."

"Yes, Holy Father. My mother is Sicilian."

"You see. I told you." He smiled and blessed me, giving me a rosary bearing his coat of arms, which he gave to all his visitors. He was so fatherly in the richest, deepest way. My heart was moved by the love that I felt when I was with him. What a grace this was for me.

Afterward, when we had all been presented, Mother Teresa hoped to detain him for a little while longer, so she sat on the floor at his feet, a Missionary of Charity custom when there are no chairs about. We immediately followed her lead and gathered around him on the floor.

"So, Holy Father," she said, looking up at him with her gleaming smile, "tell us how you love Jesus." He began to laugh. Soon, his secretary would take him by the arm and gently lead him away. His schedule was relentless. He turned and waved, offering a sweet smile that went straight into my heart.

~ ~ ~

Sister Lucy arrived in Rome six months after me, and it was a great joy to tell her of the meeting with the Holy Father. That first summer in Rome, Sister Lucy received word that her father had died back home in Montreal, Canada. I spent much time talking to her as she struggled with her vocation. She stayed and eventually became the superior of one of the convents in Haiti, working for the destitute and the dying. I eventually went home to become a teacher with a heart full of treasures—like the one I just shared with you.

I still feel the blessing of meeting the Holy Father. The orchestration of events, people, places, and time was so intricate, only God could have pulled it off. The richness of that day still leaves me in awe, feeling affirmed in God's love for me. I came to understand that sometimes our Father in Heaven wants us to experience His perfect thoughtfulness and love while we are still here on earth—a divine preview of rewards for all the little crosses we bear out of love for Him. To me, spending that morning with Pope John Paul II and Mother Teresa was as if God were saying, "Yes, my little girl, I saw the sacrifice you made, I am watching you."

They say paybacks are hell. I guess it all depends on who is paying you back.

MORNING COFFEE

There are kingdoms and cavalries

in my morning coffee;

I swirl them around with my spoon.

Forests and mountain regions

rise upward in the steam;

I sugar them with snow.

I hear

howling wolves nearing

the secret caves

where fairy legions

wage war over

the length of winter.

But my hand holds steady to the saucer.

Winter will not be overturned today.

The puppy on my lap

turns her face towards mine

with that searching puppy glance,

raised puppy brows,

and a worried lick for the tip of my nose.

"Don't worry,"

I reply aloud to her question.

"I am staying right here."

ONE-EYED SNOW CAT

One-eyed snow cat
purrs and scratches
in the snow-stiff starlit night
between the boulders
all over the shoulders
of tired old man Sunapee
deep throttle purring
keeping me awake
"Be quiet snow cat!"
one eyed winker
one eyed stinker
he won't stop
clawing through ice slabs
all hard-packed crusty
till his cat paws turn
the trails to
fresh powder, all dusty
Then
he creeps away
to sleep the day
until the icy night
when the itchy mountain
beckons through the branches
of winter trees,
"Here kitty, kitty, kitty…"

Previously published in SooNipi Magazine.
Illustration credit: Sara Tang

THE KITCHEN WALTZ

We were whisked into a kitchen waltz,
my daughter and I,
by the unavoidable ecstasy
of fresh crushed garlic
simmering
in the greenest olive oil.

We swirled
with the aroma
from room to room,
a prelude
to Sunday's second ritual:
Puccini, rigatoni and family.

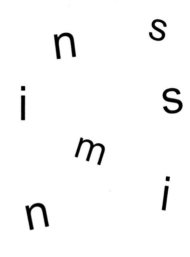

DOWN SNOWFALL

A down pillow
presses
on the summit
of Mount Sunapee;
it catches
on the needles of tall evergreens,
ripping wide open
as it passes.

Feathers fall
all over the mountain.
Now who is going to clean up this mess?

SANDPIPER MORNING

It
  was a
    sandpiper morning
      twig legs trilling like flutes
   plinking on the sand
  like the high keys
of the grand
piano

rills
  of steps
    in arpeggios
     ascending, descending
  on the silky rims of
 calm ocean
waves

gliding
  glassine waves
    that plane the rumpled sands
      into smooth sheets, temptingly untouched
    pristine pages of supple, beckoning sands
   that invite the essays
 of erudite sand
Authors

who write run on sentences with footprints and fingertips and are

paid
  in advance
    in the currency of
     seashells and the
      captivating performance
    of the song
  of a sandpiper
morning

Previously published in Kearsarge Magazine.
Illustration credit: Sara Tang

JACK TANNER, PIGMAN PRINCE

(An excerpt of a novel in progress)

This novel is about the healing power of love. It takes place in a fictitious medieval kingdom. The following chapter occurs after Jonathan, the young prince, age 11, and Sophie, age 6, the daughter of Mirra, a kitchen servant, were hurt during an attempted kidnapping. While escaping from their would-be captors, both children slammed into a brazier of burning coals. Sophie sustained serious burns on her face. The prince, whose chest was severely burned, also hit his head on the stones and became unconcious. The little girl was taken home by her mother; the royal physician is tending to the prince at the palace. The king is furious that Jonathan was not only unguarded, but was mingling with a commoner in the castle courtyard.

Chapter 5 – "Mister"

The days lingered painfully for Sophie. Mirra made a burn poultice of houseleek and comfrey leaves, laying it gently on the side of her face. Sophie rested on her cot, yielding meekly to the salves, teas, and tonics her mother concocted. Everyone knew of Mirra's skill as a healer, but no one admired her for it as much as her daughter.

Joseph had been in the fields since sunrise. It was time for the first haying. Last evening, Sophie had fallen asleep to the rhythmic sound of the sharpening stone scree, scree, screeing along the arc of the scythe blade. Her father's cheerful whistle and her mother's steady hand at the loom soothed her. It was the music of home. The curtain was drawn aside from her little cubby where she lay. Her parents' silhouettes against the firelight were a comforting distraction from the constant throb of pain on her face and in her head. She slept for long periods, waking to find her mother hovering over her, always close at hand.

On the fourth morning of Sophie's convalescence, Mirra heard a light knock at the door. She was bent over the table with pestle and mortar, blending herbs for the next poultice. Strands of dark hair escaping her coif wisped about her small face. She wiped her hands quickly, and cut some large wedges of cheese from the round on the sideboard. She hurried to wrap it in a linen cloth, and grabbed the jug of water and the loaf on the table. Before she could finish placing these in a sack, a second knock was heard.

"Now, don't be impatient," Mirra whispered to herself, "I am coming with the food. Goodness, I hope he doesn't wake my Sophie, she needs rest after such a long night! I asked Joseph to tell the men…" She glanced quickly at the figure on the cot. There was not a stir.

Mirra yanked open the door, holding out the water jug and sack of food, her lips taut, her eyes flashing with impatience. She gasped and froze for an instant, her arms outstretched. Falling to her knees before the caped figure at the door, she said, "Your Majesty, I…I…I.."

"Rise, Mirra, I must be quick. May I enter your home?" asked the Queen.

"Please…of course. You must excuse me; I was expecting the workers from the fields. Your Majesty, how is it that you are here?"

"My steward, Kenneth, brought me. He told me that your little girl was with Jonathan during the…accident." Fresh anger rose in Queen Allison's voice; a glimmer of tears rimmed her pain-filled eyes, but she would not let them fall. Turning her attention elsewhere, she collected herself. Mirra placed the victuals on the table.

"How is she?" asked the visitor, looking in the direction of the invalid on her cot.

"She is mending, and her fever seems to wane as we speak, but I am afraid there may be a terrible scar…"

"Oh, please, God, that it may not be so." Allison reached for Mirra's hands and held them in her own. "I have confidence in those hands of yours, Mirra. If anyone can work miracles, it is you. I have seen your handiwork before," said the Queen, recalling Mirra's help with an injured servant.

"I hope so, your Majesty," said Mirra.

"If the King discovers that I have come, he will be furious with me, but my son Jonathan will not be at peace until I have seen that your daughter is well. He himself is quite ill with infection, but his fever broke this morning, or I would not have dared to leave his chambers."

"Come, Your Majesty, sit by the fire," offered Mirra, as she pulled one of the hemlock benches from the trestle table and set it near the low-burning hearth.

With a gracious smile, the royal threw back her gray silk traveling cape, revealing a light brown traveling gown of simple muslin. Brown leather slippers peered out from beneath the folds of her gown as she sat.

"A cup of mead, Your Majesty?" Mirra reached for the jug of her husband's best honey wine on the shelf over the sideboard. The wooden cup escaped her grasp and danced momentarily on the sideboard before it hit the floor and rolled under the Queen's skirts. Royalty in the house at Brook Hollow was beyond Mirra's experience. She had often waited on Her Majesty in the banquet hall, but there were stewards and servants, and rules with penalties for those who would err in protocol. The informality of the Queen's visit was uncomfortable, even for a soul as sturdy as Mirra Larkrise.

Taking the cup from under her skirts, Allison handed it back to Mirra with a sympathetic smile.

"No, thank you. Do not trouble yourself over me. I come here as one mother to another. Do sit down with me, here," she patted the low stool next to her, the one Joseph used in the evenings. "It was discovered that there was an attempt to kidnap my son the night our children were together. They tried to steal my son." This time the tears escaped against her will. She quickly wiped them away.

"So that's why…," said Mirra.

"Yes, that is how the accident came about. The children were running in fear. My son should not have been out in the courtyard unattended. The King is deeply angered with the servants, with Lord Kenneth, with me," she continued. "It's not just that he was unattended, but also that he was observed behaving in a manner beneath his station, and…," the Queen paused, a flush of anger coloring her cheeks. "They are spreading rumors that the Prince is a fool, incapable of ever taking the throne."

"But they were merely children playing," said Mirra, bewildered by the complications of state.

Her Majesty rose and began to pace near the fire. It grieved her heart to recount the intrigues which embroiled the royal family.

"Lord Herrick, the King's brother, will use anything to obstruct my son from taking the throne," she turned abruptly and clasped her hands together as she spoke.

"Jonathan is held under severe scrutiny; his every move is watched. It is the burden of his station. There is no childhood for my son," said Queen Allison. A sadness swept over her. "Lord Herrick of Scarnhorst and Lord Gerund of Larsten will use any pretense to keep our regions divided and our territorial borders in dispute. They want the regions united under one King, as long as that one King is Herrick's son."

She fell silent for a moment, lost in painful thought. Coming back to herself, she sat down again next to Mirra. The Queen's eyes were a mixture of earnestness and sorrow.

"They seek my son's life, all the while making kind overtures to his father to sign peace agreements. Schemers and liars—all! If the children had not gone out to the courtyard together, this kidnapping attempt would not have been made, and your child would not be hurt," said the Queen.

"I am sorry, Your Highness," said Mirra as she fell to her knees. "Sophie is so young, I do not think she even knows who she was dancing with."

Allison took Mirra's hand and guided her to sit down again.

"What would you have me do?" said Mirra.

"My heart tells me that I must make my own plans for the safety of my son. There may come a time when I must put them into action. For now, I watch and wait." Queen Allison rose again and slowly walked about the room, lightly touching the sideboard and the mantel over the fire. She seemed so distant, as one in a dream. Suddenly, she turned with fists clenched at her sides and said, "I will not allow my son, my only surviving child, to fall into the hands of evil men. As long as I breathe, I *will* protect him."

Mirra lowered her eyes, embarrassed by the force of emotion with which the Queen spoke. Queen Allison clasped Mirra's hands in hers. Her voice held an urgency as she whispered, "There may come a day when I may, I *must* send my son Jonathan to you and your husband for safekeeping. He feels befriended by your child. Since she does not know who he is, don't tell her. They can be friends like other children, like brother and sister."

Allison sat next to Mirra. "Jonathan is heir to the throne, but I am afraid the isolation and the burden of rank will break his spirit before he comes of age. He is a different sort of a boy, sensitive, compassionate…the King cannot understand him," she said, sounding more mother than Queen. "I want to give him a chance to experience some joy and freedom before the weight of his office crushes him-- as it does to all who wear the crown." She arose, went to the window opening, and looked out over the fields, pondering.

"Would you accept my plan, if the need arises?" asked Queen Allison as she turned and reached for Mirra's hand.

"With all my heart," said Mirra as she slid onto the rushmat floor to kneel. "With all my heart," she whispered. Her upturned face was earnest and penetrating, comforting to the monarch.

"Thank you, dear Mirra. I have always seen the mother's heart in you. I know I can trust you," she said as she stood. Gesturing in the direction where Sophie lay, she said, "May I?"

"Please," said Mirra.

Allison walked quietly over to where the child lay sleeping, bent over the cot, and stroked the golden ringlets spilling from beneath Sophie's little white cap. "Poor little one," said the Queen. "Come," she motioned to Mirra. "I have a gift for her, from Jonathan." She walked with Mirra to the door of the cottage. "Jonathan feels so strongly that the accident was his fault. He insists that he will not cooperate with the doctor until I have seen Sophie with my own eyes, so I can tell him how she is, and to present her with his gift. He has such a tender heart."

Mirra followed the Queen outside to where a plain wooden carriage stood at the roadside. Lord Kenneth, the royal steward, hopped down from the driver's seat, bowing to Her Majesty as she approached. Tied to the back of the carriage was a horse, so large and majestic, Mirra could only stand and gasp at his appearance. His perfect blackness, like wet coal, was a startling sight against the summer greens of field and tree. A magnificent mane, coarse and wiry, cascaded down his powerful, high arching neck. Sunlight carved the musculature of his massive form in the curved lines of silver sheen on his black coat. Hooves as big as soup trenchers thudded as he pawed the ground.

Joseph was just returning from the fields, when he saw his wife speaking to a Lord and Lady in the yard. Drawing closer, he was startled to see that it was the Queen and the Lord Steward. He quickly took his place next to his wife, his brows raised and his mouth open to speak. She signaled him to bow and remove his cap. It was just as well that he bowed when he did because the situation was so strange to him, he could find no words to speak. He took Mirra's hand, humbly standing by her without questioning anyone.

"He is a new breed called Percheron, from the East. His name is Maiestas. It means *Majestic One*," announced the steward, as he walked over to the great horse, untying the rope that held him to the carriage. Lord Kenneth stood beside his Queen, awaiting instruction.

"The Northmen gave him as a gift to Jonathan," Allison explained to Mirra and Joseph. "They are all pomp and fineness before us—all stealth and evil behind us." She motioned to Lord Kenneth to lead the horse to Joseph. The hulking animal lumbered forward, its great hooves pounding the earth as the massive black head nodded up and down with each step.

"Jonathan sends him as a gift to Sophie. He feels responsible for her suffering," said the Queen.

"But, we could never..." Joseph, confused by these events, looked at Mirra; his implicit trust in her always ruled his decisions.

Mirra smiled and held her finger to her lips. "It will be all right," she whispered to Joseph as Lord Kenneth handed him the rope.

"I have made arrangements with the miller and the baker," the steward interjected. "You will expand the King's fields for wheat and oats. You will keep a generous amount to cover the needs of your family, and this incredible eater. You will be taxed in wheat and flour in the amount that I have instructed them. These are the King's lands; this is the King's beast. He was bred for many things, but he is not above the plow. I am sure you will find him a stout assistant in the fields," smiled Lord Kenneth. "Until the time that he begins to earn his keep, I will send you grain from the castle stables for this royal troublemaker," the steward patted Maiestas' broad shoulder.

Joseph looked up at the beautiful animal, and ran his hand along the great neck and back. The hindquarters of the horse stood high above Joseph's head.

"Maiestas," Joseph said in wonder.

Lord Kenneth then continued addressing Mirra, "The King has dismissed you from service. I'm afraid he considers you partly to blame for the harm that has come to the Prince. The King will not permit you to come back to..."

"So I have made arrangements," interrupted Queen Allison, seeing Mirra's hurt surprise, "that you may put the eastern fields of the King's property into flax for seed, oil, and the weaving of linen. Servants will be assigned to these fields to help your husband manage them. I know those magical hands are deft at spinning and at the loom," said the Queen with a broad smile. "You will make your income providing linens for the castle."

"We are in your debt, your Majesty, Lord Steward," said Joseph, bowing again, brown cap in his hands.

"It is not I, but the Queen alone that you should thank. This is Her Majesty's scheme," said Lord Kenneth, his face betraying worry.

"And the Queen will bear the consequences," said Allison, with a knowing glance to her steward. "Now, we must take our leave; any longer and I will be missed." She stepped toward the carriage. Lord Kenneth opened the door and helped the Queen inside. Leaning out, she took Mirra's hand in hers once again. "You will remember your promise to me, Mirra?"

"Yes, Your Majesty," said Mirra as she kissed the Queen's hand. Joseph bowed his deepest, holding his cap over his heart.

"One day, you will see him here," the Queen predicted, as she pulled the dark drapes across the side opening of the carriage. With a slap of the reins, Lord Kenneth urged the small brown carriage horse to turn around and head back in the direction of the castle.

Joseph and Mirra both stood staring after the carriage, overwhelmed with what had just occurred, until the stamping thud of a very large hoof broke them out of their reverie.

"I don't have a barn for, for...this," said Joseph with a gesture of exasperation toward the black mountain that shifted in front of him.

Maiestas snorted loudly, jolting Joseph to attention, causing his cap to fly off his head.

"Well, then," said Mirra, laughing, "maybe you can take him to the haying. I'm sure he can eat faster than you can scythe."

"To the house with you, woman, and leave the farming to them what knows best," said Joseph, with a smile and a quick kiss on Mirra's cheek. To Maiestas, he said,

"Come, Your Majesty, let me show you to the royal stables. We call it a barnyard. The only trouble is, there is no barn...yet." He began to whistle a tune while pulling the animal around the house to the side of Sophie's window. He thought she would enjoy the sight of the horse when she woke. He staked Maiestas near a patch of wild clover, and headed back to the men in the field.

The trailing sound of her father's whistling stirred Sophie from her sleep. She began to feel the sun's warmth on her cheek through her small window opening. Earlier, Mirra had raised the rush reed covering, to let in the light and the fresh air. Suddenly, the window went completely dark, and in the darkness a single eyeball, big and black, stared at her. *It blinked.* Sophie threw the blanket over her head, blocking it with her elbows lest it touch her burned skin; she screamed until her mother came running in from the herb garden. Moments later, Joseph burst through the door with a club in his hand, sure of an intruder. As Mirra ran to uncover Sophie, Joseph raced through the cottage and out the back door, ready for conflict, but there was no one about. Re-entering the house, he found Sophie crying in her mother's arms.

"It was big and, and, black and it had one eye...," she stopped, and reached up for her father. "Oh, Papa!" He scooped her out of bed like a feather. He now understood the cause of her fright.

"There, there, it's all right," said Joseph. "Come, my little one. I think there is someone you should meet." He carried her out the door, and around the side of the house by her window. She clung to her father's neck, her dangling feet swinging with each step. Joseph looked down at his gangly, frightened bundle, only to find her looking about with anxiety. He kissed her forehead. She snuggled into his chest. Being in her father's arms was the most secure place in the world. Suddenly, Joseph halted. Sophie sat upright.

"Ohhh...Papa, ohhhhh...," she whispered. She was entranced by the sight of the magnificent black horse.

"Beau...ti...ful," she whispered, wide-eyed. Her father gently released her. More curious than afraid, she moved toward the animal. Her small frame, covered in a thin white nightdress, proved a stark contrast to the mountainous hulk of black horse. Sophie held her arms out before her, cooing sweet words. Maiestas perked his ears, and lowered his giant head with a deep-throated purr. Sophie's tiny fingers touched his muzzle. Joseph could only stare in amazement. Turning to her father, the little girl smiled a crooked smile, forgetting the pain of her burned cheek.

"How did he get here? How...why is he here?"

"Do you remember the boy at the castle?"

"Yes, his name is Jack. He is my friend. He got hurt, too. I think he got hurt worse. I'm worried about him," she said.

"Well, he is better. He sent this horse to you as a gift. He already has a horse, and I guess he wanted you to have this one to make you feel better," explained Joseph.

"I hope his parents know about it. I know he gets in trouble a lot for doing things that they don't like."

"I think one of them knows all about it."

"What is his name, Papa?" she asked, gazing at this miraculous gift.

"Maiestas."

"Mesta?"

"Ma..ies..tas," repeated Joseph, with a patient smile.

"Mister? Oh," she said, turning back and placing both hands gently on either side of the horse's muzzle. "Mister," she said, looking up at him. "You are mine, Mister. I am going to love you. She leaned her forehead against his velvet muzzle. The pain in her face, for the moment, had disappeared.

To find out more about Susan's novel and other writings, visit her blog at www.dandelionvendor.blogspot.com.

Susan's articles have been published in *Kearsarge Magazine* and *SooNipi Magazine* and online at ourfaithinaction.org. Her favorite authors include J.R.R. Tolkien, O. Henry, and Charles Dickens.

The Prompt:

While visiting Santa Fe, I discovered the gallery of a gifted artist, who photographs abandoned vehicles in the desert, where the natural light is exceptional. I bought one of her images: a close-up of the headlight and grill of a rusted truck. It has become one of my favorite writing prompts. I display it on an easel with the simple instruction, "Write." (10 minutes) Following is Susan's response:

The Truck

I wonder when Daddy would wake up. He slept almost all afternoon. I could see his feet stickin' out from the sheets in the next room at the top of the stairs. The door never stayed shut on his room. He would slam, slam, slam it closed and, just as soon as he went to bed and pulled up the sheet, you would hear the long moany sound of it rollin' open. It was like that door had it's own mind. I won't shut because you're forcin' me, it seemed to say, I will just open a peek to be independent. The door was kinda like my daddy. He always said that he was a man of independent means. I would say, "Daddy, what is a man of independent means?" He would answer, "A man who means to be independent, like your daddy. I work hard and am beholden to no man. I takes care of myself and you kids and your mamma and don't have to take no nevermind from nobody. That's my way of life. I am pure American, you know, beholdin' to nobody in the world."

The iron bed ends both tipped towards each other when Daddy flopped into bed. The middle saggy spot was real comfortable like a hammock. Between the buzzy fly on the dusty window and the alternation of daddy's snorin', there was a little happy music to be heard 'round the house.

I surely was glad when daddy was home. I always felt safe because I knew he was safe. He worked all night long up and down the riverbed catchin' gators to sell the hides to that Yankee shoe company. I was always afraid that one night he wouldn't come home 'cause a gator got him first. So every mornin', when I come down for my oatmeal, I would listen at the top of the stairs until I could hear him snoozin'. I would catch the sound and come down the stairs smilin' breezy. This is a day without trouble.

Mamma would be there in the kitchen as she always was, elbow deep in flour, one strand of black hair hangin' forward, while the rest was pulled back tight. She hummed and worked and held conversation out loud with the Good Lord. I got most of my religion just listenin' in on those conversations.

Well, this mornin' I come to the top of the stairs and there aint no sound comin' from Daddy's room. I run over to the upstairs hall window and nope, Big Red, my Daddy's truck, wasn't in the front yard.

The Prompt:

Sometimes the simplest prompt releases the most creative writing. Visualize an edge. Free write for 5 minutes. Following is Susan's response (unedited):

The Edge

All I could remember was the hushed beauty of the sunrise on the expanse of the valley being so breathtaking that I could hardly move. Edging close on the rock at the furthermost end, I snapped photo after photo of the eerie beauty that lay in front of me. The ridgeline of treetops defined the low rills of the valley's surrounding hills pushing up to peer at the sun through the fog. The sound of stone shards tinkling down the rock face where I was perched with my camera went unheeded in the thrill of the sight of an eagle crossing the sun's face. Perfect shot. Right there … I snapped as the rock gave way and I tumbled with the boulders around me down the rock face 'till I remembered no more.

I woke to the sight of stone above me thinking hard, thinking what day, what place? The pain shooting through my leg throbbed up from my ankle. I was pinned, every part of me pinned. Then I heard the sound, unmistakable, in all of New Hampshire, the sickening shriek of the fisher.

The Prompt:

On one of my writing retreats to Italy, I asked writers to telescope in on the sensory details of a street scene in the ancient Tuscan town where we stayed. You can try this anyplace, but it was a rare treat to try it in Italy. Following is Susan's response (unedited):

The Streets of Cortona

We ramble through the village hills like children at a fair. Cobblestones and fresh crusty bread, salamis and cheeses hanging on strings and coffee cups so small, they appear as children's toys. There is kissing in the streets, cafés with table flowers, pigeons and people in equal amounts going about life simply, sated by the romance of "la vita bella." We wind our way through the ancient streets of crumbling sunlit walls with their sprawling jasmines and heavy carved doors closed on the mysteries of age-old corridors. I desperately want to peek inside. As we walk along, the climbing roses and the vistas leave me as one intoxicated. I don't know whether to whisper or shout or burst into a skip or a dance. The laughter ripples from my toes upward and rides the breezes all the way down to the valley below. Sometimes we duck inside a local church, gasping at the sweeping heights of frescoed ceilings and the passionate expression of an ardent faith in larger than life paintings and murals. I am humbled and grateful at the sight. This was their faith. It is mine, too.

These are the sights and the smells of the Italian soul. Such a different life, but my heart recognizes it. Like the sound of Pavarotti lifting the soul in the powerful crescendo of "Nessum Dorma" that steeps my heart in intense joy and pain, the beauty of Tuscany makes me suffer inside. I ask myself, how will I be able to leave this place? I recognize my home, my church, my people. These are the streets of Cortona. They have changed my heart forever.

THESAURUS ENTRY: clever
PART OF SPEECH: *adjective*
DEFINITION: showing inventiveness or originality
SYNONYMS: adept, astute, canny, cunning, foxy, keen, quick-witted, witty

Trudy

Trudy Cohen

LESS IS MORE

I began writing about 20 years ago. Short stories about my pets and a few lines of poetry would occasionally be produced, when I had some leisure time. After my husband and I moved to New Hampshire I took a writing class at a local college, and looked forward to our weekly meetings. A couple of years later, I was told about an opening in a writers' group called *Words in Play*, and decided to try going to classes again. The women in the Thursday morning group are, indeed, special, and we have a talented teacher, Deb McKew, who enjoys teaching.

Probably the most important thing I've learned about the writing process is portraying a thought or idea and making it as imposing to the reader as it is to me. The hardest thing is taking it seriously. I try to write short pieces that will draw a smile, if not make the reader laugh.

Ideas come to me sporadically when my mind is not occupied, usually while walking or driving. I'll probably continue to write as long as it doesn't become work. If it's work for me to write it, it will be work for someone to read it.

Deb's Insights:

A colleague of mine uses the expression, "just a twist of the dial." It means, look at life from a slightly different angle and maybe you can see something you couldn't see before. In other words, skew your view. No one I know does that better than Trudy.

When she first joined my workshops, she claimed that she hadn't written in years. Her first submission was a short story entitled, "Peg O' My Heart," which she had penned in 1994. She followed that story with "Let Me Call You Sweetheart," and "Happy, Happy Birthday, Baby." Her intention was to write a series of stories inspired by old song titles, but she stopped—until she joined the writing workshops. Her pieces are usually less than three pages long and often under 100 words. One day, she emailed me a dozen stories, each under 50 words. It's an addiction.

Trudy spends her days caretaking elderly people in their homes. She arranges her work schedule so she can participate in the Thursday morning writing workshop. In class, she is quiet; but if you ask her, she'll gladly tell you that she's outspoken, somewhat cynical, and opinionated. Her writing reveals her multi-faceted personality, not the least of which is her quirky sense of humor. She applies her wit and wisdom to creating stories that never fail to surprise the reader. I think she often surprises herself. That's probably what makes writing flash fiction, a specialty of hers, so much fun for her. Trudy writes for the sheer joy of the story, entertaining herself first. That's as good a reason as any I know to write.

from Trudy's Pen

LET ME CALL YOU SWEETHEART

Bea Taylor inspected her reflection in a full length mirror. "Sixty-eight years old and still a size 10," she mused.

The woman looking back at her wore a new navy silk sheath dress and matching jacket. A string of expensive pearls adorned her neck. Her ash blonde hair, still thick, was cut just below her earlobes and curled slightly under to frame her face.

Bea and her husband, Gil, had curtailed their evenings out after his stroke. She missed their active social life and tried to make up for it by volunteering where her services would do the most good. It, somehow, wasn't satisfying. She missed cocktails, dancing, and conversation.

The wedding and reception Bea and Gil were going to attend happened to be in a Methodist Church not far from their house. "Almost within walking distance," Bea said after receiving the invitation. Gil agreed to go because it promised to be a small affair and close by.

Bea picked up her handbag from their bed and entered the living room where Gil sat waiting for her. "Why did you loosen your tie?" she asked.

"I'm not feeling well. Get me an aspirin and a glass of water, would you?" Gil whispered.

Bea tossed her handbag on a table and walked quickly into the kitchen where the aspirin was kept. Her hands were shaking and she spilled the white tablets on the counter as well as the floor. She grabbed a glass from the drain board, and filled it with water from the tap. Crushing many of the little pills with her high heels, she rushed back to Gil.

Gil sat motionless, his head slumped to one side. Bea put the glass down next to him on the table and felt for a pulse. She couldn't find one in his neck or wrist. Having volunteered in a hospital, she had no doubt in her mind, Gil had passed away.

The telephone rested where she put the glass of water. She reached for it, hesitated, and didn't pick it up.

"Sweetheart, I won't be gone long. I'll tell anyone who asks that you'll be coming later. I've looked forward to this wedding for weeks; you know that. I'll call 911 when I return. I'll say I found you like this when I got home. Will it matter so much to you, Sweetheart? I didn't think so."

Bea popped the aspirin in her mouth and took a sip of water. She grabbed her handbag, retrieved the car keys from Gil's jacket pocket, and went out the front door, locking it behind her.

PEG O' MY HEART

Raymond sat in his worn out recliner, half listening to the Big Band music on the radio. He held a pencil stub in one hand, a crossword puzzle in the other. It was hot in the small, stuffy apartment; if it wasn't for the rebuilt air conditioner groaning in the living room window it would have been suffocating.

Margaret sat in an easy chair across from him, reading People Magazine, a sweating glass of Coca-Cola resting on the table at her elbow. She wore a pink housecoat and plastic flip-flops on her swollen feet. Her little toe was wrapped in a Band-Aid, and her massive calves reminded Raymond of uncooked turkey breasts. Her thin blonde hair curled tightly around her scalp; penciled eyebrows arched over pale blue, heavily mascaraed eyes, giving her a permanent look of surprise.

Raymond looked at the crossword puzzle; he hadn't penciled in one word, although he had been sitting in the same place for over an hour. His undershirt was damp and his khakis wrinkled from the humidity. Beads of perspiration, glistening on his forehead, slicked his thinning black hair.

Margaret rearranged her bulky frame. "I've got to go to the store for chopped meat and cream of chicken soup for the casserole," she remarked to Raymond.

Is she crazy? She's going to use the oven in this heat? But, all he said was, "Yes, Dear."

Margaret launched herself out of her chair and went to freshen up.

Raymond, who rarely left the apartment except for church on Sunday, sat with his head drooping slightly, eyeing the frayed carpet. He noticed Margaret's feet in his line of vision, bandaged toe and all, cramped into orthopedic sandals. His eyes traveled up her turkey legs to the cotton skirt draping her ample hips. As his gaze reached her midriff, his mouth formed a little "O" of disbelief.

Margaret had forgotten to put on her blouse; her balloon-like breasts were stuffed into a white cotton and Lycra brassiere. Raymond was about to tell her, when Margaret reached for her handbag and headed out the door.

The corners of Raymond's mouth began to curve upward. His false teeth became visible between his lips. He let out a distinct "Ha," followed by another "Ha," then a wheeze, then another "Ha, ha," then a choke, and soon Raymond was in a fit of uncontrolled laughter. When it subsided long enough for a breath, he said to himself, "The cops will arrest her for indecent exposure. They'll bring her back in a police car and serve her a summons to appear in court."

This image renewed his laughing fit. Tears spilled as he gasped for air. When the second bout of laughter subsided, he thought, "They'll commit her to an asylum where she can bake casseroles in her bra for the inmates," igniting yet another peal of laughter.

By the time Margaret returned, Raymond had regained his composure. Margaret waddled to the kitchen carrying a plastic bag in each hand, still unaware she was not fully dressed.

"Put this stuff away for me, Raymond, so I can change. It's hot as Hell out there."

Raymond stood in the kitchen putting soup cans on the shelf, singing "Peg o' My Heart" to the radio. He had sung it to Margaret many years ago.

"She never noticed she left in her underwear, and evidently no one else did, either," mused Raymond. "The store clerk probably thought she was dressed in the latest style." He started to guffaw.

Margaret, perplexed by this unusual sound coming from her husband, called to him. "What's the matter with you? You're getting stranger by the day. Don't forget to put the chopped meat in the refrigerator. You always forget something." She turned back to her magazine. "Crazy old man," she muttered.

Previously published in Kearsarge Magazine.

HAPPY, HAPPY BIRTHDAY, BABY!

Thursday afternoon Eddie Sands called his wife, Kim, from his new office. The recent promotion came with a raise in pay that allowed luxuries that had been but fantasies just months before. Kim joined a spa and started tennis lessons. Eddie bought golf clubs and planned to use them on a weekend at a 5-star resort in Connecticut. They were going to celebrate Kim's 42nd birthday in style this year.

"You're going to be late, right?" Kim said, answering the phone without saying hello.

"Yes, Babe! Jerry and I are going out for dinner. I have to get some things straight with him before the trip. I don't want to get any business calls for four days."

"Karen and I will have a bite out after doing some shopping, since you won't be home for dinner. Be prepared for a surprise. My sister took me for a complete makeover at the Blue Door. We had a great time," Kim said.

Kim usually wore her straight, light brown hair pulled into a ponytail. She used very little make-up; lip gloss and a touch of mascara were her basic cosmetic needs. In the morning, she'd put on a T-shirt, designer jeans, a pair of Nikes, and then was ready for her busy day.

"Babe, you can't improve on perfection. But, if you're shopping at *Victoria's Secret* you'd better pick up some vitamins for me."

"We'll both need them, Honey," Kim laughed.

Eddie felt less guilty knowing Kim would be with her glamorous sister. He didn't see Karen often, and when he did, she always looked different. Sometimes her hair was auburn, or dark brown. He never saw her in the same hairstyle twice, because she was never satisfied with how she looked, though Kim always referred to Karen as "the pretty one" in the family.

Eddie and Jerry chose the trendy new restaurant Dillman's. It was expensive, and highly rated by food critics.

"A definite step up from Applebee's," Eddie joked.

White tablecloths, fresh flowers, and elegant stemwear gave the establishment an air of refinement and charm. After drinking two cocktails, Eddie began to feel comfortable in the luxurious surroundings. The two men discussed business over rack of lamb and a bottle of merlot. Eddie became more relaxed after dinner, knowing Jerry was capable of looking after things while he and Kim were away.

Over Jerry's shoulder, Eddie could view the bar, where people drank their cocktails while waiting for tables. He couldn't help but notice a striking blonde take a seat. Though he was never a womanizer, and always faithful to Kim, he observed the woman with interest. She sipped her drink, holding the glass with graceful fingers that flashed long red nails. He could only see her profile, but something about her attracted him. She wore a black dress with a low V in the back. Her earlobes twinkled with diamonds, and Eddie thought, "That is one classy gal." He liked her poise. "A woman with money," he mused. He felt compelled to talk to her, a very new feeling for him.

"How about a nightcap, Jerry?" Eddie guessed Jerry would decline the offer because he faced a long drive home.

"Unlike some people, I have to work tomorrow," Jerry said, while shuffling papers in his briefcase. "Thanks for dinner, and enjoy your well deserved weekend, Ed."

The men shook hands and Jerry headed to the door. Eddie paid the check. After leaving a generous tip for the excellent service, he casually zigzagged his way between tables to the bar. He stood behind the blonde, slightly to her left. Her skin looked smooth and flawless. He wanted to touch her, but refrained. She smelled like flowers and musk, and her blonde hair had silvery highlights. It was cut short enough to reveal her neck and shoulders. Her friend, also an attractive woman, was chatting with a waiter in hopes of getting the next available table. Eddie couldn't miss the opportunity to bring his lips close to the blonde's ear.

"May I buy you a drink?" he whispered. She turned to look at him and his heart almost stopped beating. He was staring into the lovely face of his wife.

She had warned him he'd be surprised.

MOURNINGS AT SEVEN

Dan looked at the alarm clock on the end table next to his side of the bed. Almost 7 a.m.

"Miriam's awake and probably having her second cup of coffee," Dan thought, not liking the new change in Miriam's routine.

When Miriam had worked in New York City she was up at sunrise in order to make her daily commute. After retirement, Dan and Miriam enjoyed the luxury of sleeping later and having breakfast together. The recent shift in Miriam's morning custom didn't concern Dan except for one occasion when he had entered the kitchen and found his wife reading the morning paper, sipping a mug of coffee, and smoking a cigarette. Astonished, he'd said, "Miriam, what are you doing?"

She shrugged her shoulders and crushed the remains of her cigarette in a saucer. It wasn't mentioned again.

Dan punched his pillow and rolled over, snuggling in for another hour or so of rest. He heard a noise, but couldn't define it, at first. Then he realized it was Miriam.

"Ooooh! Ooooh, no!" she wailed.

Dan threw the covers off and got out of bed as quickly as his arthritic legs allowed. He hastened to the bathroom, knocked, and entered.

"Miriam, Miriam," he called breathlessly.

His wife stood in front of the bathroom mirror dressed in a navy blue business suit. Comb in hand, she turned and looked at him with such anguish, Dan could only stare.

"My hair, my hair. Andre over-bleached my hair. I can't go to the office like this. He's going to have to color it my regular shade," she cried, tears streaming down her face.

Dan stood looking at her with his mouth open. He almost said, "Miriam, have you gone crazy?"

But, she had. Her hair had been the same silvery gray for over 30 years.

HONEY BUN

Alice Kane removed her ample body from the pillow on which she had sat for a full 15 minutes. It wasn't a comfortable position. Her feet dangled off the bed and she had to balance herself by holding on to the headboard.

She now sat, catching her breath, on a straight back bedroom chair. She looked at her husband lying motionless. The pillow, residing inside a floral print pillowcase, covered his face and head; the indentation from where she had sat retained the curve of her backside.

"Well, Ralph," she whispered, "my fat ass was good for something."

Alice arose slowly and removed the pillow from Ralph's balding head. She then slipped back into bed next to her husband.

~ ~ ~

Alice Finch and Ralph Kane were married, against her mother's wishes, in a simple ceremony. "He doesn't treat you with respect, Alice. You'll have a miserable life with the jerk," her mother warned. "I can't imagine what you see in him. He's not well educated, no manners, and his eyes are too close together."

Alice, after only a few months of wedlock, knew her mother was right. She didn't want to give her mother the satisfaction of saying, "I told you so," so she suffered in silence.

Ralph, always critical and a nit-picker, found fault with everything Alice did. Even though she kept a tidy house, cooked a savory dinner every night, tended the garden, and carefully looked after their only child, Grace, Ralph managed to find something to complain about.

A few weeks prior to Alice's liberation, she overheard Ralph say to the mailman, Elmer Reeves, "Yah, that Mrs. Norstrom, across the street there, has some trim, tight, little figure on her. She's about Alice's age, too. Guess she don't eat those honey buns like Alice does. Yah, Mrs. Norstrom bendin' over and weedin' the garden is a sight to behold. Alice, here, is not only increasin' the size of her fat ass, she's gettin' funny in the noggin', too." Ralph tapped his finger against his temple. Shaking his head with contempt, a tight-lipped Mr. Reeves walked to his next stop.

Ralph began talking to Grace about her mother, too. "She's gettin' senile, Gracie. You know your old Dad can't handle anything like that. If she keeps on, I'll put 'er in a home. Yah, I can't deal with that kinda stuff."

"I haven't noticed that Mom's any different, but it could be coming on gradually. Maybe she's just having a bad spell," Grace said, patting his hand.

~ ~ ~

Alice slept like the dead. She woke up at her regular time, got out of bed, and checked on Ralph. Not breathing. *Good.* She called her daughter's cell phone.

"Gracie, Daddy's dead. He died in his sleep. Can you come over?"

Several hours later, Alice and Grace sat drinking coffee at Alice's kitchen table. A red and white checked table cloth was a cheery addition to the sunny, immaculate breakfast nook. Alice wore her elastic waisted, blue poplin pants. Her pink cotton tee shirt featured a white kitten motif. Her short hair curled around her plump cheeks, giving her the look of a cherub.

"I killed Daddy," Alice confided.

"Oh, Mom, don't say things like that. Somebody might hear it and believe you. Dr. Wills said he died of natural causes."

Alice looked at her daughter with a blank expression. She was off the hook.

"Mom, if you'll be all right for a couple of hours, I'll see to things at the funeral home. Do you want me to ask Mrs. Norstrom to stay with you?"

"No, not that woman," she thought, but said, "No, Dear, I'll be all right."

Grace gave her mother a gentle kiss on the cheek. She closed the kitchen door quietly and departed to take care of sad and unpleasant duties. Alice lingered at the table, thinking that Mrs. Norstron had probably already eaten her half cup of Special K with skim milk, and walked the three miles to and from the bridge, as she did every morning, to keep her figure youthful. With that in mind, Alice poured another cup of coffee with plenty of cream and placed two honey buns on her plate. She smiled with satisfaction.

"After a suitable amount of time, perhaps Mr. Reeves would like to join me for a cup of coffee and a honey bun. Heard he lost his wife about a year ago. He's such a nice man," Alice mused, as she chewed the first of her delectable morning treats.

THE KISS

On a rainy morning, we were to meet for a late breakfast. Jeff arrived first and was waiting for me under the overhang of a local restaurant, trying to stay dry. I dashed from my car; he had the door open before I reached him.

We get together on a regular basis for lunch, a movie, sometimes dinner or cocktails. I certainly don't consider our relationship a romance, but I always greet him with a kiss and a hug. It just seems natural, although I'm the one who initiates the action.

"The weatherman didn't predict this," Jeff said as we entered the dining room.

We found a quiet table where we could talk, and ordered breakfast. When we finished eating our eggs and bacon, we lingered over coffee, neither of us in any rush to face the damp, gray day. Jeff mentioned he had brought along a book I had asked to borrow.

"It's not raining very hard now; my car is parked close by, if you want to get the book," Jeff said.

"Yes, I'm anxious to read it," I replied.

Jeff paid the cashier and we prepared to face the elements. I wore a fleece jacket, not waterproof, but I didn't think I'd be out too long. We walked to Jeff's car and he unlocked the door. The book was wrapped in a plastic bag, safe from the rain, which had become heavier.

"Thanks, I'll return it as soon as I can," I said, turning to leave. I took only a couple of steps and when I glanced back, Jeff was still standing by the car door, not making any move to get in. He stood in the rain, looking at me. We were both getting soaked, but I quickly retraced my steps and gave him his awaited kiss.

My hair wet and jacket damp, I sat behind the wheel of my car, oddly touched by Jeff's sentimentality. Somehow, it made me feel melancholy; my eyes stung with rain water, or maybe tears.

Knickers in a Twist

"Oh, no," Allison Nickerson groaned to herself. Her smooth brow furrowed, and her full lips turned down when she spied Bobby. She squeezed her brown eyes tightly shut, hoping when she opened them, he'd be gone. "I hate this kid. I have him in class all week, and now he's invaded my weekend."

Bobby always seemed to demand attention, which left her frazzled at the end of the day. He couldn't seem to sit still, used his "outdoor voice" constantly, and never had a sick day.

With a partially filled shopping cart, Allison stood in the canned soup aisle. When Bobby found her, he galloped in her direction at full speed.

"Hi, Mrs. Knickers," he called out excitedly.

"Bobby, I want you to call me Ms. Nickerson. That is my name. I don't want to keep correcting you on that," Allison stated crossly.

Bobby wiped the back of his hand over his runny nose, and shrugged his narrow shoulders. His red hair needed cutting, and his freckled face and blue tee shirt were dirty from reckless play. "You sure like that kind of soup," he observed.

In error, Allison had placed six cans of Italian wedding soup in her cart, while distracted by Bobby. "Good grief! One can of chicken with rice was all I wanted," she thought. "I refuse to put the cans back in front of the little menace. I'd rather buy them, than let him see I made a mistake."

Allison shopped at the P&C supermarket every Saturday morning. She always bought just what she needed for the week, usually making her selections carefully. She'd never married, thanks to Barney Grady, who had dumped her after a three-year engagement. Tall, slender, and blessed with dark curly hair, Allison dated occasionally, but never found anyone she liked better than Barney. She decided to devote her time and energy to teaching because she loved children, in general. This year, however, brought Bobby Sparks.

"Bobby, where is your mother?"

Hopping from one leg to the other and waving his arms like a windmill, he replied, "She's at the check-out counter."

"Let's join her," Allison said. Although she hadn't finished her shopping, she wanted to get away from Bobby quickly.

At the check-out, a young man packed up Allison's few purchases, but paid more attention to the tattooed cashier, with her purple tipped hair, than to his task at hand; he loaded all six large cans into one flimsy plastic bag. Allison would have asked for double bagging if she wasn't in such a hurry to leave. She wheeled her cart quickly out the door. There was no sign of Mrs. Sparks.

Bobby trotted along behind her, singing a tuneless song, his body in perpetual motion. Allison popped the trunk of her VW and began hastily to put her groceries inside. As she hefted the bag containing soup cans, the plastic bottom gave way, and all six cans of Italian wedding soup made their getaway. Rolling down a slight incline, each can took a different direction for escape. One aimed for safety under a Pontiac Vibe, but Bobby was on it, quick as a cat. Before it stopped rolling, the boy, on his belly, reached under the car and grabbed the can. Up in a flash, he retrieved another lodged next to a truck tire. The third rested under a shopping cart. He ran back to Allison, handed her the cans; off again to run down the remaining three. One can, almost crushed by an SUV survived undamaged due to Bobby's intervention. He found the two remaining cans huddled together against the curb.

"Thank you," Allison said, slightly awed. "You were very helpful, indeed."

From between cars, Mrs. Sparks approached. She had seen her heroic son help his school teacher in an emergency, and beamed with pride.

"It would not have been easy picking up those cans in a dress," said Allison to Bobby's mother.

"My husband and I want Bobby to be polite and respectful," Mrs. Sparks said seriously. "And, we try to teach him good manners."

Allison looked closely at Mrs. Sparks to see if she was joking. She wasn't.

Allison reached into the trunk of her VW and selected a reward for Bobby. As soon as she handed him the candy bar, she realized her mistake. He looked at the wrapper, grinned broadly, and in a sing-song voice began his new chant: "Mrs. Knickers loves to eat Snickers…No, no. Mrs. Knickers will only eat Snickers…"

"I hate that kid," Allison thought as she got into the sanctuary of her car.

EUGENE

Emma Wren had a nice job, thanks to her deceased husband's employer, Mr. Rice. She cleaned bathrooms at night at the American Agricultural Laboratory in Perkinsville, Ohio, a 15-minute drive from the house she had once shared with her pale, overweight, listless husband.

Emma never missed being on the job at 9:00 p.m., although no one cared what hours she kept, as long as the bathrooms were cleaned and stocked with paper products. Her husband had been a devoted employee, and his computer expertise had played an important part in the growth of AAL.

Emma knew Mr. Rice had thought highly of her husband, so she did not hesitate asking him for a job. She needed to go back to work in order to make ends meet.

"If we don't have an opening, we'll create a position for you," Mr. Rice promised.

True to his word, Mr. Rice found Emma a job; she began cleaning the bathrooms (two on each of three floors) in the square, brick building that was home to the AAL. Emma's routine hadn't changed much after her husband's death. She continued visiting her sister, bowling weekly, watching soap operas, and tending to her elaborate variety of houseplants. Watering her indoor exotic garden took hours.

It wasn't any wonder that Emma looked forward to being employed. She felt useful and important. She had her very own key to the employee entrance and since there wasn't a security guard, she felt that that was also her job, though unofficially.

On this particular night, she arrived just before 9 o'clock, unlocked the heavy door and proceeded to the utility room to collect supplies (bucket, mop, rags, sponges and disinfectant). She hung up her sweater and changed her outside shoes to Keds sneakers, an action similar to Mr. Rogers', a host of a popular children's TV show. Emma took the elevator to the third-floor executive bathrooms. All bathrooms were located in the main hallways. Emma never saw the offices, meeting rooms, or the laboratories, where her husband devoted so much of his time. AAL developed pesticides and insecticides. It was also rumored that they bred "super" bugs—insects that were resistant to the chemicals that were currently used in agriculture.

Emma entered the first bathroom and began her methodical chores. It was during her last task, mopping the dark green tiled floor, when she noticed milky trails, little slimy paths that seemed to emerge from under the sink. Her eyes followed the path of sticky lines, eventually focusing on a pink head with tentacles, attached to a spongy, pink body about two inches long. The pair of eyes on the ends of its tentacles seemed to be looking at her. It was a slug, but its color was not the common gray of the garden variety. Something familiar in its movements compelled her to watch the little critter. From the wastebasket, she retrieved remains of a BLT; she removed the tomato and lettuce and offered it to the slimy creature.

She completed her work in the other bathrooms, then came back to finish up, giving the slug time to eat in peace. When she returned to the top floor bathroom, the scraps were gone. The slug was waiting for her, or so it seemed to Emma. The thought never once entered her mind to flush the slug down the toilet.

"You remind me of someone once close to me," she said. "I'm going to name you Eugene, after my husband. Until tomorrow, Eugene."

The following night, Emma arrived with lettuce, strawberries, and an overripe pear.

Eugene was waiting for her and she presented the gifts to him. He appeared to be larger than he was the night before. His milky trails were wider, too. Even if he wasn't discovered during the day (slugs are nocturnal), the paths would be noticed. She attended to her work and came back to clean up after Eugene.

"Eugene," Emma whispered. "You can't stay here. Tomorrow is my night off but I'll be back to take you home."

Eugene slowly glided away on his path of mucus to his hiding place under the sink. Emma turned off the lights and walked to her car.

Saturday morning Emma woke earlier than usual. She showered, dried her short dark hair, dressed in jeans and a tee shirt and began a plan to change her lonely life. The first stop on her list: a pet store, where she purchased a pet carrier. Next, she went to the supermarket for produce and fruit, then to WalMart Garden Center for bark mulch. Having completed the shopping, Emma spent the rest of the day clearing a place under her kitchen sink and bedding it down with bark mulch. Saturday night, Emma drove to AAL only to find Mr. Rice's car parked in his designated spot. She now was in a state of panic. "He probably came to take care of unfinished work. He could be anywhere, but I'm here to claim Eugene, and I won't leave without him," Emma said to herself defiantly. "I'm going in."

She entered the building and headed to the third floor. From under Mr. Rice's door, she saw light seeping into the gloomy hallway. She knocked gingerly, and said, "Mr. Rice? It's me, Emma."

Mr. Rice opened the door and said with surprise, "What brings you to AAL on your evening off?"

"Mr. Rice, I'm very sorry to disturb you, but I've been looking all day for my wristwatch," Emma lied. "I came to see if it might be in the utility room. I saw your car and I just wanted to make sure you were okay before I left."

"I'm ready to leave, myself," he said with a smile. "Can I help you look?"

"No, no," Emma said, too quickly. "Er, I don't want to put you to any trouble, and I know where to find it, if it's here," she said trying to calm herself.

"All right," he replied.

After Mr. Rice closed his door, Emma swiftly made her way out to her car for the pet carrier. She then hastened to Eugene's bathroom, but he wasn't waiting.

"Eugene," she whispered. "Come out."

Eugene didn't like the desperation in her voice. The nervous actions of his friend made him feel insecure.

"Mr. Rice can come in here, anytime," Emma pleaded.

No sooner were the words out of her mouth, when she heard Mr. Rice's footsteps coming down the hall. Emma put the pet carrier on a toilet seat in one of the stalls. She had just enough time to turn the water on in the sink, as Mr. Rice opened the door.

"Excuse me, Emma," he blushed with embarrassment.

"I'm sorry to be in here, Mr. Rice, but I needed the bathroom in a hurry. I'm going to stay here just a few minutes until my stomach settles," she said.

Mr. Rice, not wanting to get involved said, "I hope you feel better. Good night!" and closed the door with haste.

Emma rested her back against the tile wall and sank to a sitting position. A long soft sigh released the tension from her body, and Eugene stuck his head out from under the sink. Emma smiled at Eugene as he made his way toward her on his foot. His curled skirt, a darker pink than his tail, looked like a petticoat. He was growing, no doubt about it.

Emma retrieved the carrier, and for the first time touched Eugene. He was sticky. She put him safely in the carrier. Before leaving she cleaned up the slime produced by his pedal gland and washed her hands.

Eugene grew to the size of a Chihuahua in a matter of months. Emma was amazed, and worried. She thought he must be aging quickly, too. He was genetically altered, which would account for his color, size, and intelligence.

During the afternoons, Emma would put on a raincoat backwards, sit in her faux leather recliner. Eugene would sit on her lap, and together, they'd watch soaps and

Oprah. When Emma had a busy day, Eugene retired to his home under the kitchen sink, leaving Emma free to shop and do errands.

One day after visiting her sister, Emma came home to find her house plants knocked off the sills, pots broken, and plants crushed on the floor—in general, a disaster area. Only Eugene could have caused it; most unusual behavior for her stoic friend. However, she made other disturbing observations. Eugene's color wasn't as vivid. His appetite was off, too. What could Emma do? Taking him to the vet was out of the question.

One afternoon, weeks after the plant episode, while watching *Days of Our Lives* together, Eugene passed away. They were sitting on the recliner, Emma's hand resting on Eugene's mantle, when she felt his life force leave him. He went quietly, like he did everything. Emma cried for Eugene…a second time.

The slug, Eugene, was buried in the back yard in a bed of cosmos that he would probably have eaten if he'd been allowed out. Emma continued her routine of working and visiting her sister. She was existing; not happy, not unhappy. She didn't realize her state of mind until one day, while tending to her plants, she noticed the leaves of her zebra plants had been chewed. She discovered the culprit was a little pink slug.

Emma couldn't have been more thrilled if she had won the lottery. "I'll name you Ray, after Mr. Rice. It can be for either a male or female. I never dreamed Eugene was a Eugenie."

AN EPISODE AT GEM POND

My mother's health began declining many months before my father died. Dr. Edgar, Mother's neurologist, spoke to me candidly during one of our many visits. He perched on the corner of his polished desk, holding Mother's medical records, and looked seriously into my eyes.

"Ms. Stanton, Pearl, we know your mother suffers from Parkinson's. This is complicated by her diabetes and dementia. She stayed strong because your father needed her. Now, your mother is going to need you, and I hope you'll be up for the task," he said doubtfully. "It's going to be a very hard job."

Dr. Edgar did not mention my problem with depression. I knew it was on his mind, and I could see the concern in his eyes regarding my capabilities. Being an only child, it would be up to me to make my mother as comfortable as possible in her declining years. I undertook the challenge with confidence and enthusiasm, at first.

I moved into the little cape Mother and Dad had once shared. Originally a waterfront summer home, it had been winterized, and they lived there all year after I "left the nest."

In my childhood, I loved the house, even though it smelled of mildew and dampness. The small windows didn't allow sun and warmth access to the dark interior, but we welcomed its coolness during hot summer months. The kitchen, a mismatched affair, revealed badly worn flooring created by years of being trod on by sandaled feet and snow-covered boots. The appliances were not replaced because they still performed, though not as well as they once did. Mother and Dad lived in harmony with each other, the natural beauty of the outdoors, and Gem Pond.

The first few months flew by as I prepared the cottage to accommodate my mother. A hospital bed replaced my parents' double bed, and a TV was mounted to the wall. Furniture was removed from the living room to allow more space for a wheelchair. Bathroom facilities were modified so Mother could use the toilet and sink easily. I regretted that Dr. Edgar couldn't see, with his disapproving eyes, how professionally I handled every detail.

As weeks melted into months, it began to look like a nursing home. And, it began to smell like one: disinfectant, urine, and baby powder. Every day my chores became more overwhelming. Laundry, cooking, bathing, medications, cleaning; when Mother could no longer talk, the loneliness became unbearable.

Usually after lunch, while Mother napped, I allowed myself the luxury of an hour outside to enjoy fresh air and a short walk to the boat ramp. After my father had retired, he had one built. He fished almost every day from a little motor boat, so the ramp had plenty of use.

On one particularly warm spring day, I found myself envious of people canoeing and fishing. I watched them leisurely paddle near the shore or cast their lines into the calm water. As the days began to grow longer, I yearned for the summer when I would be able to open windows and replace stale air with gentle, clean breezes. The change in weather might make Mother feel better, too. She hadn't been eating, and it was becoming more difficult for her to manage.

After my short walk, I went back to the house, elated. Why couldn't I bring Mother out, in her wheelchair? It would be a pleasant change from our usual routine, and I desperately wanted to be outside longer. As I entered the kitchen, my eyes adjusted to the darkness. I made my way to Mother's room, and moved the wheel chair next to her bed, locking the wheels. I placed bedroom slippers over her socks, wrapped her in a soft, fleece blanket, and sat her in the chair. I had difficulty getting her seated and lifting her feet onto the foot rests. She seemed inflexible and resistant.

Soon, I began wheeling her out the door and into the sunshine. Her thin, stiff fingers clutched the light blue blanket. In the light of day, her skin, like paper, had a yellowish cast, which I hadn't noticed indoors. I wheeled her toward the boat ramp, bumping her lightly over tufts of new grass, and soft earth. Beads of perspiration formed on my forehead and upper lip from the exertion, and the sun's warmth.

"Are you doing OK?" I asked. I stopped to look at her face. Her eyes were half closed and glassy. Her mouth was slack, he lips dry, and she wore a pained expression on her wrinkled face. "This isn't going well," I thought. "She's certain to curtail this little bit of pleasure, make me take her back to the house, even though it's a glorious day."

We began again to move forward on the lumpy grass. I looked down at her white hair, so sparse it didn't cover her scalp. When we reached the boat ramp I didn't stop. I kept pushing the chair forward, easier now that we were on the cement decline. I pushed the chair into the pale green water. It felt delicious on my tired feet. It cooled my lower legs. As it rose over Mothers knees, I continued to push the chair farther into the pond. Up to my thighs, it covered her lap, now to her waist, and then her chest. The water reached below my breasts, and turned the blanket dark blue, where it became soaked. Little sparkling rings of water began to rise quickly around the loose flesh on her neck.

Suddenly, like a large bass breaking the surface with a splash, Mother's arms appeared from under the saturated blanket. Over her shoulders, she reached back at me. Her fingers gripped like talons of a large bird. She grabbed my chest, her thumbs digging into my breasts as she screamed like a parrot, "Pearl, you bitch!" My blouse tore and shredded into ribbons, as though slashed by an angry cat.

I came back to reality in a state of panic, like waking from a nightmare. Why were we in the water? What had happened? I pulled the wheelchair backwards, up the ramp, made more difficult because of the weight of the blanket and Mother's struggling. My shoes kept slipping, making it hard to gain traction. When we were free of the water, I dislodged Mother from her chair and carried her, like a bridegroom carries his bride over the threshold. She seemed light as a feather. Both of us dripping, we entered the kitchen, its musty smell assaulting me. I placed her on the bed, and dried her with towels. After dressing her in a clean nightgown, I covered her thin, limp body with an extra blanket. Her eyes were shut, her mouth closed. She looked comfortable and serene.

My hands quivering, I retrieved a bra and panties from my dresser. I found denim pants and a shirt from a stack of laundry I had yet to fold. Quickly, I went to the bathroom to change. I stood naked drying my body. My ribs protruded under stretched skin; my hip bones were prominent on either side of a deflated belly. I put on my bra, but it hung from my shoulders. The underpants drooped between my thighs. I slipped on jeans and a tee shirt that were several sizes too large. When was the last time I showered or changed my clothes? Have I been eating? Looking in the mirror I didn't know the person staring back at me. Black circles etched under puffy eyes, and hair, stringy and long, hung on the sides of sunken cheeks. Now distraught, I heard myself whimpering.

I needed dry shoes and found a pair of sneakers in my closet. I hastily laced them up with shaking hands. I had to get the wheelchair and wet blanket from near the boat ramp. I walked into the kitchen and was startled to see two dark figures standing outside the storm door. The sun, behind the intruders, made it impossible for me to recognize them. A knock came, loud and commanding. Fumbling with the handle, I managed to open the door. Two police officers stood before me in starched blue uniforms. A tall, young blonde man and a woman with dark hair, looked at me with empty faces.

"May we come in?" the man asked.

I stepped aside, and he entered first. The woman stood unobtrusively next to him.

"Ms. Stanton?" he inquired.

I wanted to tell him about the episode involving me and my mother, but I couldn't speak. My legs began to weaken. He pulled a chair out for me, and gently held my elbow so I could sit without losing my balance.

"Do you need a drink of water?" He didn't wait for a reply, but took a glass from the drain board and filled it half full with tap water. He handed it to me, and I drank thirstily. I wanted more, and licked every drop from my lips, but he didn't give me any, and I couldn't ask for it.

The woman had quietly walked into Mother's room, and came back a few minutes later.

"We received a report that there appeared to be an incident by the lake a little while ago. Do you know what that's about?"

I opened my mouth, closed it and opened it again, like a fish gasping for life in the bottom of my father's boat.

"She's dead," the dark haired woman whispered.

I couldn't understand who she was talking about. Maybe she meant me.

~ ~ ~

I raised my head after hearing Dr. Greenberg open the door. He slowly walked across the gray carpet and took his place in a black leather swivel chair behind his massive mahogany desk. He didn't look at me until he was seated. It's one of his many quirks. He peered over his reading glasses at me, and smiled like a craftsman who is satisfied with a work in progress. Tall, thin, and nattily attired, Dr. Greenberg is a prominent psychiatrist.

"Hello, Pearl."

"Hello, Dr. Greenberg."

"How are you feeling today?" It's a question he never forgets to ask.

"I'm well, but I'm hungry, and looking forward to lunch," I answered.

"It's gratifying to hear you have a good appetite." He smiled briefly before continuing, "Last week, I mentioned we would be breaking new ground at this session. Shall we begin?"

"If you think I'm ready, I'll do my best," I answered.

"You don't remember what happened after the police officers spoke to you on the day of the episode; you just remember waking up one morning and being here, at Fairfield Manor. I'm going to fill in the blanks for you today, Pearl," he said, while reviewing his notes. "It will all become clearer in the months ahead."

It comforted me to know that I'd be here for a long while, because I never want to leave the Manor. I eat well, my clothes are washed, my room is bright, clean, and spacious; I even have friends. The grounds are beautifully kept, and I can walk outside as often as I like. We do crafts and play cards. Mother left me enough in her estate to allow me to receive treatment here. She had been frugal, and invested wisely.

"Pearl, the police called an ambulance to take you to hospital. You were examined and found to be undernourished, dehydrated, and anemic. Now, you told me that your mother grabbed your chest, cutting into you with her nails, and also tore your blouse. I know this is going to be a difficult concept for you to grasp, but no marks were found on your chest, shoulders, or breasts. Your blouse was not damaged."

"That can't be. Why would I lie about such a thing?" I said, my voice rising.

"No, Pearl, I don't, for one moment, think you would lie to me. But, because of your physical condition, you were probably hallucinating."

"She didn't grab me? She didn't scream at me?"

"It was impossible for her to do that. When the autopsy was done on your mother, it was determined that she had been dead at least two days, maybe three, before the episode," he said.

I leaned forward in my chair, my hands grasping the armrests with white knuckles. I felt my heart beat wildly, and my mouth opened for more air. The gray carpet began to undulate, rising and falling in gentle swells. I looked down at my feet and saw the carpeting had turned to pond water. Little wavelets were lapping at my suede flats. I pulled my feet back in an effort to keep them dry.

"Pearl, sit back and take a deep breath. Let it out slowly. I know this is difficult, but we'll get through it," Dr. Greenberg said.

I sat back, exhaled, and closed my eyes. When I opened them again, the water started to recede and the swells ceased.

"Are you all right, Pearl?"

"Yes, I think so. Are we having baked chicken for lunch today? It's my favorite," I said.

"It's almost lunch time, and I think we've covered enough for now," Dr. Greenberg said.

I rose from my chair and walked slowly toward the door. I turned and smiled benignly. "Good-bye, Dr. Greenberg." I closed the door securely behind me, leaving Dr. Greenberg, and my mother, in his office until next Tuesday.

SHORT SHORTS

HOT AND STRONG

How can I explain? It's like not thinking about coffee until you smell the tantalizing aroma on a cold morning; then you can't think of anything else. A steaming cup of delicious caffeine is irresistible. After your departure, I deleted you from my mind. I didn't think of you. Then you came back without warning and memories of the past began to percolate. In less time than it took to brew a pot of coffee, you again became my addiction.

READING TEA LEAVES

"Postpone your vacation. I see you in a debilitating accident." My fortuneteller replaced her teacup reverently back in its saucer.

Rushing to the travel agency to cancel, I tripped on a discarded umbrella and broke my wrist.

Dr. Kumar advised me to postpone my vacation.

CASINO LOGIC

"What? I'm not about to spend $40 for a sweatshirt!"

"You're right, Honey," I said shivering. "They're not worth more than $12. I'll buy a hot cup of coffee. That will warm me up."

"Good thinking! Then, let's try the $5 slots. Maybe we'll have better luck," my husband said.

STOOD UP

Last Friday Rita waited for his call. Dressed in tight jeans, huge hoop earrings and big hair, she was ready for a hot date. He didn't call. Tonight she's hoping fervently he'll phone. She wants the satisfaction of not answering.

PET OWNERSHIP

Open can, feed dog. Let cat in. Let dog out. Open can, feed cat. Let dog in. Cat tosses tuna. Let cat out. Dog is on sofa. Let dog out. Let dog in. Let cat in. Open can, feed dog. Let dog out. Open can, feed cat.

MOTHER'S MY ONLY GIRL

"Not to worry, mom," I said knowingly. "I won't fall for the first co-ed I meet. I won't succumb to the lures of glamorous city women. I won't get a girl pregnant. Believe me, mom, while I'm away at college I'll have a gay old time without the ladies."

EXACTLY

My 8-year-old playmate looked at my new sweater with envy.

"I've got one exactly like it," she said, "Exactly, except my buttons are white, and it's a darker blue with short sleeves. Other than that, it's exactly the same."

Trudy's stories have been published in *Kearsarge Magazine.* In addition, she has submitted her flash fiction to numerous contests and she has won several prizes for them. Her favorite authors include Tom Wolfe, Kinky Friedman, Stephen King, and James Patterson.

Invitation to Play

The Prompt:

As a teacher, my role is to encourage students to tap into their creativity by providing many and varied opportunities for inspiration to occur. To that end, I took my writing group on a field trip one day to Lake Sunapee's yacht club. It was a dreary, rainy day, but I sent the writers outside to absorb the atmosphere and reflect on a character and how that character might respond to the scene before her. The writers then returned inside and wrote for 10 minutes. Trudy's response (which became the inspiration for her featured story, "An Episode at Gem Pond"):

Mood Indigo

An hour or two a day to myself is all I get. Taking a little time for solitude at the lake, I find my mood fits the dismal landscape. I observe a gray horizon. Whitish fog, like Mother's hair, thin, dry looking and wispy, finds hiding places in nooks and crannies in distant mountains. It's a flat, metallic lake today disturbed only by tiny raindrops and the silver circles they produce.

Water drips from a bathhouse over-hang, sounding like Mother peeing in her portable toilet. How long can she last? Ninety-two and still demanding my time, my energy, my freedom.

I imagine pushing Mother's head under the lake's shiny surface. My hands securely on her fragile shoulders, her white hair swirling just below the water, like seaweed. Her bony bird-like body struggling briefly before submitting to a long, restful sleep, freeing me from my nightmare of offensive smells, drudgery and loneliness.

Today's outing is not a refreshing change in routine. It is but a mirror image of my life.

The Prompt:

I chose to include several responses to the artistic photograph of an old truck because the responses were so unique. Here is Trudy's interpretation of the prompt to write in response to the artistic photo of a rusted, old truck. (10 minutes)

Truck

Shiny, new, a state-of-the-art sculpture more than pleasing to the eye. My grandpa looked at the truck with wonder, and a warm glow of anticipation. He saved his money diligently for the purchase of this 1947 yellow beauty. His heart's desire, Grandpa felt an attachment, a bond. . .like the truck was a new lady in his life. A someone, not an "it," that would surround him with warmth on a cold day, propel him to adventures he couldn't imagine, be faithful and beautiful. All the qualities not present in Grandma.

The Prompt:

Colors are wonderful prompts. You can use the same colors every day and each time something new emerges. Here is what Trudy wrote when she was prompted to write about the color Red:

Red

It was hot…the color of candy apples, intense and shiny, glossy and sexy. The vintage sports car would soon be Jerry's; the dream of a lifetime and mechanical equivalent to Gwen Stefani. How lucky could an 18 year old guy be to have such a machine to fulfill his utmost fantasy? It represented freedom, a babe magnate, and the envy of every motor head in the state. To sit behind the wheel of a truly awesome engineering marvel left him with only one word on his lips: the word for a future license plate: HOT.

Bobbi

Roberta Baldwin Stoneman

THE HERE AND NOW, AND REMEMBERING WHEN

Cape Cod in the 1930s and '40s was an idyllic place to grow up. The tapestry of my life then was woven of many threads in nature's colors: blue of sky and ocean, beige of sandy beaches, green of scrub pine woods, grey of clouds and fog, brown of dogs and farm animals.

The youngest of four, I was willful and independent; I learned to swim, sail and ride horses by age 9. My sister and I spent summer hours reading, exploring, bird watching, bike riding, enjoying family picnics and playing games like Parcheesi and Mah Jong. We attended small schools and summer camps that fostered creative writing, geography, music, and outdoor activities.

111

One of the many great things about the *Words in Play* workshops is meeting other writers, sharing our work out loud in a supportive, helpful climate that often includes many laughs, along with some tears.

We have learned how important it is to have constructive and thoughtful feedback from everyone, but most of all to have an instructor who "knows her stuff" and continues to challenge each of us. I've learned specifics—dialogue, theme, setting, plot, character development, and more. The free writing prompts motivate me to think outside my box in personal essays and short stories.

Writing my memoir has been a long process. I need and want to explore memories of my sister, our family, our homes, our Cape Cod adventures. Sometimes, the writing flows as smoothly as an incoming tide sliding over sandflats; other times, it is more like slashing storm waves shifting the contours of the shoreline.

Newly revealed memories still delight me...a forgotten dialogue, a cousin's long-ago tennis victory, my one-time hole-in-one, the name of my first palomino, the smell of my dad's leather jacket. Pen to paper makes the magic happen.

Deb's Insights:

The very first writing exercise I presented in my creative writing workshops was to describe a bathroom. That's all—simply write about any bathroom. The assumption was that most would write in broad strokes, and I would then ask them to return to that room and revise their descriptions using specific details that would inspire a particular mood.

When Bobbi read her initial response, I could sense a bit of awe in the room. She transported us to a bathroom in an old house that she knew well; cracks in the porcelain fixtures were like spider's webs, a faint smell of talcum and ivory soap lingered, the uneven floorboards revealed its age. At that moment, I realized two things: I could not assume anything; and I loved teaching writing.

Bobbi has consistently participated in my workshops over the years. She recreates a place vividly, her characters seem to lift off the page into the room, she incorporates specific sensory detail to engage the reader, and she has many stories to tell.

What Bobbi lacked, initially, was a focus. She thought she might write a book about the house that was the cornerstone of her life on the Cape. She had given this much thought, hence the vivid detail of that bathroom. As time went on, Bobbi started to write more about the people who surrounded her youth, in particular, her older sister, Mimmy. Her stories started to take on a life of their own. In the process of writing, even during class exercises, we all began to see a pattern. Bobbi's detour from writing about a physical place that held fond memories led her to writing about a sister she had lost long ago, which led her to an understanding about herself and her need to untangle the complex relationships within her family. Through it all she has learned that truth has many facets; the process for her has been cathartic.

Bobbi's first memoir is nearly complete, and I do believe her next one will be about the big old house whose rooms still have stories to tell.

from Bobbi's Pen

SERVED HIM RIGHT

Late one hot afternoon, our kitchen window screeched up and Mother called, "Girls…time to come in…I need you now!" She set the prop stick back in place to keep the window open.

I was 7; Mimmy was 12. "We're coming!" Side by side we trudged up the hill from the creek, sharing the bale of our full bucket so heavy it dented our hands. Wading in the cool tumble of water to scoop up eels and snails with a bent colander felt so good that we made ourselves late for our favorite chore—helping Mother prepare fish chowder. Our brother Jake and sister Jane liked Friday suppers best and bragged about what good cooks we were.

Dad, however, was harder to please. No matter how hard Mother worked, or what she prepared—meat loaf, stew or even lamb chops—Dad never told her whether he liked it or not. He'd smile at each of us, ensconce himself in his captain's chair with a freshly popped bottle of Schlitz, rest his Spud cigarette on the edge of a clamshell, clear his throat, cough, scratch, eat, belch, but make no comment.

This particular Friday he seemed grumpy. No smile, just a grunting, "Well? Where are my cooks? I'm hungry!"

Jake ducked his head, carefully cleaning his fingernails with a penknife. Jane fussed, folding and refolding our blue and white woven napkins. No one argued with Dad's cello voice.

"Oh, now, don't take on so, we're nearly finished, dear," Mother soothed, even though it wasn't quite true.

"Yes, yes, just joshing you a bit," Dad popped another icy bottle. He tried so hard to make us, his not-very-appreciative children, laugh with his "not-very-funny-Dad!"

jokes, pranks, or teasing. Now that he had new dentures, or "choppers" as he affectionately called them, he loved to irritate us by flipping them in and out with his tongue. But on long car trips, he played endless word games to challenge us. If Mimmy or I caught his glance in the rear-view mirror, he'd begin, "If the plural of mouse is mice, why isn't the plural of house, hice? How about goose/geese or moose/meese? Your turn, you do one!" He'd chuckle the miles away.

Now, at the dinner table, well, wouldn't it be bad manners to joke or "josh," especially with Mother, so what was he thinking?

Mimmy and I hurriedly peeled and sliced onions and potatoes, cut them into thumb-sized chunks, got out the milk, butter, and slabs of snow-white codfish, then lined up everything on the counter. Two loaves of crusty white bread, fresh from the oven, breathed softly on the windowsill.

"Do you think Daddy will like this batch, Mother?" Mimmy asked. "Billy Nelson just caught the cod this morning. Smell how fresh it is! He told me it's sweet as salt air."

"No, Dodo," I said, giving her an elbow poke. "What he really said was, 'as sweet as running down the beach at low tide with your mouth open.'"

"Indeed! Well, we'll see, dear," said Mother. "Your father usually doesn't say anything about his food, good or bad, you know that. Why, sometimes I think he wouldn't notice if I served him an old dishrag!"

"I could probably toss in some of these eels and snails," Mimmy said, holding up our bucket, "and he'd never know."

"Wouldn't surprise me a bit," Mother agreed. "But cross as he is tonight, I'd tread gently. Those new teeth of his must be too tight!"

Every Friday night in summer was comfortingly the same. Blue-edged chowder bowls, shiny soup spoons, hunks of bread, and butter curls floating in a wooden bowl of ice water were all neatly arranged on woven blue and white placemats. Usually, after Mother ladled Dad's chowder from the wide-hipped tureen into his own bowl, the tureen was covered with a domed lid to keep the soup steaming hot. Usually, we all waited until Dad said grace, then, soon as he'd lifted the lid, we could begin.

But that one time, that particular Friday night, when Mother said "Just start in, Dad's is a bit special tonight," no one waited. Jake and Jane slurped up their first spoonful and said, "Mmmm," and "Great batch, Mother!" but kept their heads down, not wanting to meet Dad's glower.

Mimmy and I blew on our bowls to cool the chowder a bit. Mother, making little sneezing sounds and muffled snorts as if trying not to giggle, kept getting up to go into the kitchen for one thing or another—first salt, then sliced tomatoes, then more bread. Finally, she brought in Dad's chowder serving.

Dad lifted the dome, set it in front of him. He dipped his spoon into his deep bowl…paused…looked down…looked up at Mimmy, then at me, finally at Mother, whose eyes twinkled even as she held her breath.

"What's this?" he said, quietly, and then very loudly, "WHAT IS THIS? Which cooks are to blame for this slop?"

There it lay, a steaming gray mass neatly piled. It really was a boiled dishrag right in the middle of the milk in his bowl. It even had a lump of butter melting on its peak.

Jake snorted. Jane ducked her head, smirking. Had they been in on the secret?

"I didn't do it, I promise it wasn't me," Mimmy said, beginning to cry. I wanted to smack her! She was always whimpering when Dad frowned.

But would he be angry? Would he slam stuff around? Would he pull off his wide leather belt like last week when Jake shouted that Jane was a bitch?

"Why, John, for pity's sake, is there something wrong with your chowder?" Mother stifled a laugh, then exclaimed softly, "I wonder how in the world that got there!" Then she smiled, and continued to calmly spoon up her own soup.

Jake and Jane laughed out loud! How did they dare? Wouldn't Dad be furious?

But no, he took a deep breath, got up, carried the mess to the kitchen sink, hitched up his dungarees, came back, sat down, opened another beer, lit another cigarette, rubbed his belly, grinned at Mother, then said, "Point well taken, Mary dear. Well done."

Then patting me and Mimmy gently on our hands said, "Outstanding chowda, girls, and the best ever!"

ASPIC

Mother cherished many sayings and phrases to guide her through the intricacies of family life. Many of her favorite sayings related to food.

The clean plate club had not been invented back then, thank goodness, but if I or my sisters carefully tucked a few flabby, over-cooked string beans beneath a fold of mashed potatoes on the far corner of our Blue Willow plate, we were admonished to, "Remember the starving Synovians!"

"Who are the starving Synovians, Mother?" I whined.

"Never mind dear, just eat and be grateful."

What did Mother do after suppers, scoop our leftovers into a package and mail it to them?

One hot summer night in Bar Harbor, when I was perhaps 8 years old, we were having a family dinner at Grandma Fenno's, and Delia, her maid, had served each of us something square of an orangey-red color that just lay there, shivering on a side plate, nestled on one perfect leaf of Bibb lettuce. I had never seen anything like it before.

Mimmy, my next oldest sister, pushed her plate closer to mine, trying to pretend it did not even belong to her. I bonked my elbow into hers. I was not about to eat anything that moved like that wiggly red stuff.

Jane, older still and always doing the right thing, let her salad fork slide right into her square; she ate it all without even flinching. Her eyes stared right into mine as she did so, daring me to laugh.

Grandma was enjoying hers as well, taking teeny little bites with a teeny little fork, as she always did, ever so delicately.

"What is it?" I whispered to Mimmy.

"I have not a clue!" she fussed. "But, I'm sending mine to those starving guys!"

"Girls!" Mother was frowning.

Uh-oh, there was another one coming.

"Waste not, want not!" said Mother. "Eat hearty, give the house a good name!"

I really wanted to eat just the lamb chop, asparagus and scalloped potatoes, and leave that jittery red stuff way over there. It made me nervous just looking at it!

"Mother, what is it?" Mimmy was brave enough to ask, sounding polite, but only delaying the moment when she had to actually put it in her mouth. She'd probably have one of her nosebleeds, if Mother insisted.

Daddy consumed his in two mouthfuls, then got busy smearing mint jelly on his chop, from bone edge to crispy fat.

"It is called aspic, Mimmy dear—*tomahtoe* aspic," said Grandma. "It has tomahtoes, and celery, and tomahtoe juice in it. Here, put some mayonnaise dressing on it."

Aspic? What a weird name; it sounded like a garden tool! So, it was like cold tomato soup? Tomato jello? Oh, no…

Well, now they were all looking at me and Mimmy. She usually got to do things before I did and collected the praise for being so smart and musical. Maybe, just this once…

I looked over at Daddy's smile. His eyebrows were telling me, "Go on, go on, you can do it!"

So, I daubed a nice blob of mayonnaise on top of the aspic, spooned into it, closed my eyes, and took a big bite, rolling it around in my mouth the way Tigger had tried with haycorns.

Hmmmmm...

Cool and salty, it tasted like ripe garden fruit and crispy green celery stalks, and it slid right down my throat in a sort of friendly way!

Aspic...I liked it!

Mimmy was glowering at me..."Traitor!" she hissed.

Those starving Synovians (whoever they were) would have to go hungry one more night—they were not going to get MY aspic!

HUARACHES - 1943

"They just need breaking in, so stop picking on me," Mimmy said, pacing back and forth, back and forth, between kitchen and dining room.

"Okay, okay, calm down, sweetheart," Daddy said, breaking up his toast into the five-minute egg Mother had prepared. "Meanwhile, why not take them off for a bit and give us all a break? Or, go outdoors and toughen up your soles like Mabs does?"

Every summer, once school was out, I tossed my brown lace-ups in the back of my closet and practiced marching up and down our clamshell driveway barefoot and skipping along hot sidewalks. The bottoms of my feet were thick and tough as dog paws. I could even walk over broken glass!

"Oh, no, Daddy," said Mimmy. "That might hurt. I can't."

"Well, just run along, then. Leave me in peace."

"Sissy. Crybaby. You just have to practice." Each time I said it, she probably hated me even more. We had good times playing duets together on our piano, but she wouldn't even try roller skating with me for fear of bloody knees.

After a rain, or when Mimmy's feet sweat, those new huaraches smelled like wet straw. Or a horse's stall that needed cleaning. After being dried in the sun, they squeaked with every step, as if a mouse's tail had been stepped on. But Mimmy loved her shoes and that year, her eleventh summer, she wore them every day. Barefoot. No socks, ever. This made her feet blistered and swampy.

Her huaraches made her imagine Mexico, that fantasy land of pepitas, nachos, and tortillas; she practiced saying those magical words over and over just in case she could go there someday.

"I know about these places," she waved one of Daddy's *National Geographic* magazines at me. "I can just see a little senora with long black hair, squatting in front of her hogan, weaving baskets and sandals out of straw to earn some pesos for her family."

"Sitting in the boiling sun wearing a striped serape, I suppose?" I chimed in to the dream talk I had heard so many times.

"Oh, yes, yes—with a clay oven just outside, and five or six dogs and goats wandering in her front yard. Wouldn't that be wonderful?"

"I'd rather have a horse."

Mimmy could never go anywhere in our house without each of us being aware of her presence; the sound of her shoes gave her away. She missed out on so much! She never overheard any family secrets. Never crouched behind the sofa or tip-toed along the hallways or crept into our brother Jake's forbidden darkroom to peek at his private photographs clothespin-clipped to a string over the sink. I could even slide along the kitchen floor behind Mrs. Annie Robinson when she was decorating a cake, swipe a lick of frosting, then slink away without her knowing.

~ ~ ~

That was the summer when our grown-up cousin, Margo, was getting married.

"A nice girl with a big heart," Mother had said, hulling berries and pursing her lips. "Too bad she's so homely. I wonder what that Paul fellow sees in her."

"If you ask me it might be that she sails, plays great tennis, and don't forget those big bazoomers, too!" said Jake, snatching a huge strawberry to suck on as he passed through our kitchen.

"Well, I didn't ask you—what a wicked mind you have, son!"

Margo planned to be married in St. Mary's church just down the road from our house. Everyone in our family and everyone in the village was invited. It would be a celebration to remember, with frothy gowns, green and yellow ribbons, and balloons everywhere. Even the old family car, Uncle Wims' Marmon, would overflow with flowers for the ceremony.

What to wear to this, the biggest happening of our summer? Mother loved planning "outfits" for a family event. She took all three of her daughters—Jane, Mimmy, and me—on an all-day shopping spree in Boston. At Bonwit's, Jordan Marsh, and Filene's, we tried on flowery frocks in daffodil colors and crinoline hats with wide brims and perky bows.

I loved the gowns best. Not for me to wear, thank goodness, because they itched and squeezed my middle, but to stare at Mother and Jane's silky apricot underwear as they pulled the dresses off and on, then twirled in front of long mirrors in narrow rooms that smelled of Arrid deodorant and rose water. Mimmy and I dreamed of someday wearing camisoles and step-ins after outgrowing our cotton Lollipop briefs and undershirts. But for Margo's wedding, we knew we'd be outfitted in the yellow-flowered dirndl skirts and white puffy-sleeved blouses that Mrs. Annie Robinson had made, which already hung in our closets. At least we got to shop at Leen's Shoes for black patent leather Capezios.

"I won't wear them," Mimmy whined, "not now, not ever. They're baby shoes."

"Don't fuss, dearie," Mother said. "You certainly may not wear those huaraches you've got on!"

"Yes, I can, too."

"No, you may not. The whole congregation would hear you squeaking up the aisle instead of the lovely organ music."

"I don't care. I won't go. You can't make me."

"We'll see about that! What would people say if one of my girls stayed home?"

"Don't care. Won't go."

"Oh shut up, Mimmy," snapped Jane. "It's not your wedding. Besides, you don't get to choose your outfits until you get the curse and need a bra. That's the rule."

I just stood there, listening to them argue. I hugged my new shoes in their pink striped box, then lifted the lid to stroke the patent leather, cool and slick as licorice. No one noticed.

When Margo's wedding day finally arrived, it was a blistering August afternoon. Dad trimmed his mustache and fingernails, and polished his specs; he looked handsome in his seersucker suit. Mother, dressed in navy blue organza, wore two camellias pinned to her waist. Jane looked pretty in her halter-top floral print dress with its bolero jacket. Mimmy and I were shampooed, combed and curled; we even carried white gloves. The shine of my new shoes was perfect! Mimmy, wearing her huaraches, promised to don her new shoes, which she carried in a grocery sack, at the church entrance. A few early guests had wandered in to the shadowed pews indoors, but a big crowd lined the walkway, fanning themselves with hankies, waiting for bridesmaids and bride to appear.

Suddenly, down the hill to our right, its horn blaring "Aruuuugah," came the flower-filled Marmon, with Margo in front clutching her veil, blinking against the bright sun. Uncle Wims, father of the bride, was at the wheel, his shiny forehead lobster red, a cigarette drooping from the corner of his mouth. When he hopped out of his car with a huge grin, Mother gasped, "Oh, for pity's sake! What was he thinking?"

Everyone who had gathered outside the church gasped, then began to point, whisper, and laugh. Uncle Wims was wearing white Bermuda shorts, navy knee socks, madras jacket, cummerbund, and bow tie. I thought he looked snazzy and very proud! His bowlegs, hairy and tanned, looked like cup handles. They were all everyone noticed, for in the congregation, a crowd of friends and family, women giggled, men snorted.

"Shorts in our church!"

"Unheard of!"

"Shocking!"

"Well, I never!"

The church bells rang.

The best man dashed out, top hat askew, cutaway flying, flapping his long arms to herd everyone into their pews; he signaled the organist to begin. Mimmy, with no time to switch shoes, squeaked into our pew. No one heard the squeaks. Everyone was too amazed as Margo, beaming, her hand on her father's arm, glided down the aisle over smithereens of confetti. Her lipstick was perfect, her shoulders tanned, her bouquet firmly held to her waist.

Whispers chased through the church like skittering mice:

"Why, she really looks beautiful!"

"At long last. Thank you, Lord."

"Will wonders never cease?"

"Love can do miracles."

Everyone sang every hymn. We all hushed to hear Margo and Paul speak their promises of love. Mother sniffled into her hanky. Mimmy and I both slid our shoes off and stroked the velvet kneeling pads with our bare toes. Jane uncurled and recurled a lock of her hair, imagining herself in a white gown one day.

After the "pronounce you man and wife" part, Uncle Wims turned with a huge grin, the look in his eyes daring anyone to say a rude word. But, something had changed, something wonderful had happened. Things that were important, shone; everything else—a little girl in squeaky shoes, a grown man's bare legs in church—was milkweed fluff, easily blown away.

STICKS AND STONES

For two months after Daddy died, Mother took to her bed with "the vapors," so Aunty Hope vowed to raise my sister, Mimmy, and me.

I was 10, an age relatives called "obedient but mischievous." Mimmy, at 15, was a "worrisome girl given to nosebleeds."

We were terrified of Aunty Hope's deep voice, the riding crop in her left hand, and the orders she snapped at the dogs, her cleaning lady, and us. Hard as we tried, it was impossible to please her.

"Come here! Stand straight!" Her words stung like wasps.

"Yes, ma'm," I said. Mimmy pressed her lips tight.

"First thing is to get you girls into decent shape. Seems like you're carrying huge inner tubes around your bellies. I won't be seen at the yacht club with chubby relatives. Here!"

She handed us two cardboard tubes. "Put them on under your bathing suits. I'll be in my car."

Pepto-Bismol pink and smelling like new tennis balls, the things collapsed in our hands like stretchy rubber pancakes. We read the instructions on the label: "Liberally dust your body and the inside of your new Playtex Living Girdle with talcum. Roll smoothly from knees to waist and behold the new, slender you."

Mimmy and I struggled to pull up first one side, then the other, of our jelly-fish contraptions. Garters hugged our thighs like tentacles.

"What if I can't do it?" I cried. "Aunty Hope will never stop nagging about it. I can't breathe; my skin is suffocating!"

Mimmy tugged and jerked, then minced over to her long mirror. "Oh, great, now I am flat, but it is fat flat! Aunty's mean and she's wrong!" Mimmy ripped the girdle off, "I won't care what she says, not ever."

"Neither will I," I resolved. "Never ever!"

The car horn bleated. Twice.

Previously published in Here in Hanover *magazine.*

LADY LIMULUS

I love you, Lady Limulus, aged underwater queen,
with helmet jeweled by barnacles.
For decades you safely scuffled over pleated sand,
a wooden salad bowl on tiptoes.
Your only foe th'insistent tug of shallow tides,
you'd thread your way through rocky pools
from shore to ocean's edge.
Until, alas, some sunburned hooligans
snatched you from beneath a wave,
flipped you over into hot sun
on this hot beach,
and you became this helpless
turvied horseshoe crab,
legs tap-dancing the sky
like tanned hands that beg for help:
a baked potato,
an acorn squash, sliced clean in half
and headed for the oven.
But look, the tide is in, I've found you just in time!

❧

TURTLE WATCH

I lay on my stomach on the sand, watching the gentle incoming tide for any sign of narrow then flaring nostrils, the top of a huge head, black sand-dollar eyes, or a greenish, blackish lumpy carapace.

No wind, no lights except the jitter of our Earthwatch rescue team's flashlights far down Ten-Mile Beach. Stars hung so low they tore jagged holes in an indigo sky, the Southern Cross hummed just out of reach. Smooth tropical waves whispered in, pulled back, pulsed ever closer to the wrack line by my feet.

My partner for the watch, Charlotte, called out, "Here she comes!"

"Quiet, shhhh — just wait."

As salt water streamed from the grooves on her back, our evening's first leatherback turtle, a living, breathing fossil the size of a small car, emerged. Charlotte and I sat motionless, not wanting to frighten her from her mission.

Slowly, but with lumbering grace and gigantic effort, she flippered her way out of the water, bringing the musk of seaweed at low tide. Her head, a scaly, oval melon, bobbled up and down as our lady peered towards her goal of secluded beach beyond the berm. She gasped, then huffed and puffed up, up, up, the slanted beach, sliding on her smooth plastron toward the scraggly bushes beyond us. Could she make it that far? Would she be safe? As she went by, I reached out to touch her back, firm but slippery as my dad's leather jacket.

We were to measure and tag her as part of EarthWatch's *Save the Leatherback Project*. We were to describe exactly how she excavated the hole she needed as a nest, and catch and count the slippery eggs, the size of ping-pong balls, that would plop from under her triangular tail. If possible, we would also photograph her, being careful to keep the flash from disorienting her.

Eventually we wanted to be sure she made her way back to the water without getting stuck in roots of those bushes, and without being misguided by hotel lights shimmering on the horizon. If she started to crawl towards the hotel instead of the water, we were to turn her 900-pound body around, quickly!

The worst possible scenario? We might have to defend her, and her nest of precious eggs, from poachers who were probably lurking just out of sight. This part of Sandy Point, St. Croix, was to become a protected habitat, but meanwhile, we had been warned that many two-legged shadows crouched in the dark, waiting.

The poachers, native Cruzans, knew it was illegal to steal the eggs, but they also knew they could sell each one in the streets for 5 dollars, especially to the men who believed sucking a raw turtle egg would make them virile.

Once our lady leatherback found the spot where she would begin her excavating, Charlotte and I began to examine her, careful to stay behind her line of sight. She looked to be about eight feet long and three feet high, with well developed front flippers, strong enough to accidentally break my leg if I moved too close. Her left rear flipper, however, was merely a stub.

"Probably a shark did that," said Charlotte. "At least she got away."

"But she needs her rear flippers to dig out her nest hole, one scoop of sand at a time," I said. "I wonder how she has managed."

The front flippers were meant to sweep sand back over the nest after all the eggs had been released. The smell and feel of the sand against her belly must have finally felt right, so she began. Because of the damage, our lady's task became Sisyphean—every time she dug with the stubby right flipper to pull sand out, the left one pushed sand back in. While Charlotte clipped the metal tag on a front flipper, measured and photographed, I knelt down behind the turtle, scooping out the sand that ought to have been the left flipper's job. Here was a beautiful, barnacle-encrusted, enormous creature working so hard to follow her ancient instincts, and now I could actually help in her process! What a gift. She grunted and dug, I sweated and swatted at hordes of bloodthirsty no-see-ums, biting in spite of the layers of oily Skin-So-Soft that was supposed to bug-proof my exposed skin.

Our lady turtle used her back flippers to test the depth of her nest hole. First, the right one paused its scooping, reached into the hole, wiggled a bit and, feeling only air, stopped. The broken left back flipper performed the same action and as it also felt only air, thanks to my frantic hand shoveling, both stopped scooping.

The turtle sighed deeply, grunted, lifted her tail a fraction; out came the slippery ping-pong balls—one, one, one, three, four at a time. I could hardly keep up with the count. Counting in clumps of five, I estimated the number of eggs sliding through my fingers like moist, tan canvas spheres that hardened almost immediately as they nestled in the hole. Fifty-five, ninety, one-hundred-thirty eggs piled up before the last two dribbled out. Immediately, the front flippers went into frantic action, like swiveling oars swishing sand back, back and back again, over the nest. I stroked her warm grooved and knobby carapace, the texture of a convertible's top or leather books left out in the rain. I could feel her breathe! I patted her neck, wet and scaly, yet smooth and pulsing with her efforts.

Finally it was over. Charlotte measured the width of the flippers' reach, known as "wispy to wispy." Nine feet! We stood back and watched our lady humping and heaving herself over the little berm between the bushes. Unable to back up, she slowly turned around, focused on the ocean's horizon, and headed back to sea. As the first wave of the receding tide flushed sand from her face, she paused for one more breath. Then, she plowed her head down and, under the next wave, disappeared into deep darkness.

Charlotte and I both waved and cried as our turtle swam away. Such an effort! How huge and magnificent was her body! Would she return once more this nesting season, to lay another clutch of baby turtles to incubate until June? Perhaps. Then someone could record her tag number and keep tabs on her. Unless the poachers got hungry for turtle soup.

A dark shape, then three, approached us, bare feet shuffling in the squeaky sand.

"Hey! Missy, you okay?"

Oh, God, what if they're the poachers? Charlotte and I sat on a beach towel spread protectively over the top of the egg nest.

"Missus?" Flashlight shone into our faces!

"Get up, sista!"

"No, I'm tired. Go away," growled Charlotte.

"Who are you?" I managed, sounding fierce, but scared enough to gag. After all our turtle's work, I would be damned if I'd give up protecting the eggs.

"Hey, here be me, Nicodemus, see?" He shined the light on his own bearded face. Indeed it was, our hero!

Nicodemus, the six-foot-nine-inch, 300-pound native forest ranger (in this case beach ranger), stood with a rifle in each hand, and a couple of handguns in his belt, flanked by his buddies, who also carried rifles.

"Jeeesh! You scared the shit out of us!" Charlotte steamed.

"Aw, I hope not for real, lady," Nicodemus chuckled. "Don't want to cite you for littering our good beach, ya know."

Nicodemus and his mute side-kicks squatted down, lit cigars to fend off bugs, and gazed out to sea.

Our teammates, Scott and Karen, appeared from behind the scraggly berm, looking concerned, then relieved, as they recognized our company. With Nicodemus around, we were totally safe. He chortled, telling how he had just stalked and arrested a gang of "dem bad foke poachers" on the other inlet of the beach, and how they were handcuffed to a dune buggy on their way to jail.

"You best call it a night now—dawn soon be coming," Nicodemus suggested. "My boys and me patrol until then."

And so we did, knowing the beach was protected at least one more night.

LEATHERBACK MOTHER

Full of 80 eggs, creamy, slick as golf balls,
she heaves up-beach at full moon tide,
then dredges out a hole, making sand fly.
Shadowed pirates watch and creep in closer.
She moans and grunts, then lumbers back to sea.
Tomorrow, plunderers will market her unhatched babies.
Instinct tells her, try another beach.

THE NOTE

It was just a piece of rain-smeared, blue-lined notebook paper stuck on the front door of Brad's dorm, but it stabbed me like an icicle. My name wasn't on it, but I knew it was meant for me. Those wide, shaky letters printed with a black marker commanded me to "Go Home."

That was all. No other words. Just "Go Home." Not even an "I'm sorry." Bastard!

He must have tacked it right over the peep hole late the night before, blinking fast, trying to stay awake, drunk from all the frat party beer, teetering in his boots like a wind-blown gull clutching a buoy at mid-tide. And it must have been after two a.m., or Gus would have taken the note down, tossed it away as he made his final rounds. Gus liked to protect "his boys" from girls trying to sneak in after hours. It was not allowed, certainly not on his beat!

Hadn't Brad and I been having a rare time at the party, drinking, dancing, teasing each other on the shaggy brown sofa by the fireplace? Why hadn't he warned me when he dropped me off at curfew? Now, here it was, Sunday, dawn of Dartmouth Winter Carnival, and there I was, cold and alone. What about those romantic plans? What about huddling under his striped Hudson blanket, sipping sherry and listening to Harry Belafonte as we had done the month before, celebrating his 19th birthday? How could I have known the dreams I'd been spinning for the two of us were only real in my head. Fool.

And where was "home"? Where did he really want me to go? Back to Mrs. Hall's boarding house, where I slept for the weekend, or back on the train to Boston? How would I get to White River at this hour? No one else was up on campus. No huddled figure in parka and stadium boots bent over, resisting what was turning into sleet needles blown straight from Canada.

It was still dark when I left my room at six. Mrs. Hall, her faded yellow chenille robe tied with a tasseled curtain pull, met me with coffee and cigarette, whispering, "Who's there? Anything wrong?"

In jeans and heavy sweater, I carried my duffle and tried to creep out ever so quietly, but as a housemother, Mrs. Hall was prepared to protect "her" girls even if she only hosted us for a night or two.

"Just me, Mrs. Hall, I'm catching the next train. Thanks, and goodbye!"

"Oh, well, be careful, dearie, don't let your heart break into too many pieces!" Wise woman, she must have seen all this many times.

I shuffled up the slushy sidewalk toward Hanover center, where lights from the Inn smiled out its front windows, crooning "Come in. Come in and be warm."

Thank goodness the coffee shop was open all night. Maybe I could take a cab to the station, or catch a ride with one of the guests.

Seven a.m. I checked the train schedule posted behind the coffee counter. Leave White River at 11, arrive North Station at 3. I sat on one of the tippy wooden chairs with a round seat no bigger than a dinner plate and creaky curly back support. Gladys was there as usual, forking up bacon on the grill, filling up the decaf and cocoa pitchers. Her green apron was clean, but her hair was all bed-snarled, her green fingernail polish nearly chipped off. She hummed to herself, keeping her back to me. Sleet tap-danced on the window, thickening, turning to snow.

"Gladys, do you have any doughnuts out yet? Cinnamon ones, maybe?"

"Do you see any out here, hon? No? Too early I'd say. What's wrong? Why are you crying?"

"I got flushed. Brad's hung-over again or worse. Probably sick of me now. Told me to leave."

"Yeah? They're like that, these kids. Think they're all grown up; big fellas when they're in bed, don'cha know, but get all scared when the L word is mentioned. Didn't tell him you loved him, did'ya?"

I nodded and blew my nose.

"Big mistake. Can't handle it. Here, have a stick of bacon on toast. Who you waiting on, now, anyway?"

"Thanks. Anyone who'll give me a ride, I guess."

"Ha. Good luck. Way early. Wicked cold out, too. Those boys won't be up `til noon." Gladys went through swinging doors marked YES and NO, disappeared in the back kitchen, still humming. Then her radio came on; I could hear Elvis Presley chanting "Heartbreak Hotel."

A tall figure went by the window, all dark green parka and white woolly cap, bent against the wind and swirl of snow; he paused, rubbing a mitten on the glass to see in. He had black hair, black mustache, a big smile. He pushed the door open shaking the snow off his head and whuffling like an Irish wolfhound. Thank God, someone I knew, someone I could trust—Shamus, Brad's best friend.

"Hey! I thought it was you in here! What are you doing? Where's Brad?"

"Oh, crap, he flushed me. Look." I pulled out the crumpled, soggy notebook paper from my pocket and thrust it at Shamus.

"That bastard." Shamus dropped his parka on the floor, unwound his green and white striped scarf and tucked it around my neck and shoulders. He hugged me warm and tight. "You are way too good for him. I'm sorry, though, I know you liked him a lot, huh?"

He smelled like wet wool, soap, and peanut butter. I sobbed into his plaid shirt, and blew my nose in a wad of napkins from the shiny holder on the counter.

"Damn him, anyway; what did I do wrong?"

"Not a thing, babe, not a blessed thing. I know him, he does this, has done it before. I could have warned you but it wasn't my place, see. But now I can tell you not to hurt yourself over him."

"Too late. I feel like I've been ground up and shoved aside by a snowplow."

"Then, I'll be here to pick up the scraps, OK?"

Gladys returned, now humming Elvis's tune, "Just give me some lovin, baby…uh-huh…"

"Suppose you want coffee too, eh, Shamus?" Gladys knew all the college boys, especially the nice ones.

He grinned at her. What a great smile; it made his blue eyes turn to cobalt. "Sure, I'd be grateful."

We stayed in the coffee shop, knees bumping under the wire-legged table, until nearly ten. A few hotel guests wandered in, looked out, yanked up coat collars, and forged out into blowing snow to go watch the ski jumping event. The doughnuts came, chocolate covered and cinnamon sugared. Shamus bought me one of each , broke off chunks and fed them to me, all the time talking, soothing, whispering about an exam he was studying for, a movie he'd like to see, a bike race in April he was training for.

When it was time to leave for the train, he stood up and took my hand. "Come on, I'll ride the bus there with you, just to be sure you make it."

As the train chuffed to the platform, Shamus tucked the ends of his scarf under my jacket. "Keep it. At least wear it for now, you need it more than I do and I like thinking of it keeping you warm when I can't."

"Really? You sure?" I hugged him. Having a college scarf to go back to my dorm with was almost like being pinned. Well, almost. The best part was he cared about me. The notebook paper was in the trash back at the coffee shop. Pain from icicle stab had melted away.

"I'm sure. And I will call you soon." He stood very close, pressing his chilled fingertips on my hot cheeks.

Then, gently, warmly, he kissed me—cinnamon crumbs, snowflakes, and all. I tasted him all the way back to Boston.

RACE POINT

This most northern spit of sand
claims me!
Here, winter waves crack open sapphires
that remind me of his eyes,
and cold wind rakes its hands
across the dunes
through harsh yellow grass
unruly as his hair, just out of bed.

He always did that, after making love,
shake his head, grin,
then push those big tanned hands
from forehead to neck
and laugh
as loud as waves that rush the shore.
Oh! None of these footprints
here now are his. Not one!
Yet though the sea, the sky,
yes, even the entire beach seems empty,
he is here to touch me
with every wave,
and cloud
and shell
and grain of sand.

Previously published in Kearsarge Magazine.

PEAK EXPERIENCE

He was ideal—tall, lean-legged, strong and blond with enormous, gentle eyes. The moment he stepped into the barn that July morning, I knew my search was over. Against my neck his warm breath smelled of molasses. Eagerly, I stroked his wide chest, dark with sweat.

At last, the perfect palomino quarter horse gelding! Ever since I'd envisioned Trigger rearing up and whinnying, I'd dreamed of my very own palomino. Long before, for my eleventh birthday, Aunty Hope had given me a small mare, Blond Taffy, that I kept in Mr. Ben Crocker's barn on Cape Cod. Pale as hominy grits, she was sweet and gentle and I rode her as often as I could beg Mother to drive me to Mr. Ben's. Mr. Ben, a retired jockey, had a loud, scary voice. But he taught me well. His motto was: "gentle hands, firm legs."

Sadly, by the time I was 13, I had grown too tall and too heavy for my Taffy. Mr. Ben took her in exchange for free riding lessons. When my family moved to Boston, so I could go to school, I had no chance to ride. But I never stopped wanting to own my own horse.

Now, at 34, I lived in Illinois, and as soon as my youngest was in kindergarten I had found Mr. G.'s eight-stall stable.

"Yup, I found your yellow horse," Mr. G. Grinned. "What do you think?"

To label the glorious beast dancing around on the end of a lead rope "yellow" was an insult! His coat gleamed gold, his mane and tail flared like sun-bleached hay.

"He looks smart and strong. Thanks."

"Yeah. He's a good one."

"Is he broke?"

"Only to halter. He was used at stud but couldn't sire foals in true color so they cut him to sell. You're gonna have to work on him."

Since my divorce, I'd worked in Mr. G.'s stable nearly a year, grooming, cleaning and exercising his horses. I worked in exchange for board and lessons. He was the most gifted horseman I'd ever seen. Whether walking, riding, adjusting someone's stirrup leathers or simply running his hands up and down a horse's legs feeling for bruises, his body was gracefully in balance. Although he never seemed to notice, I was wildly, stupidly in love with Jay Grayson, with his onyx eyes, Aramis cologne, flexible hands and long legs. He was totally consumed with his love of horses; buying, selling, training and showing them. Totally unavailable. But maybe I could change his mind if I was clever enough. He'd spent months looking for a pleasure horse for me to train and I trusted his judgment, still, I had to be sure. Would the right questions keep his attention, keep him from walking away?

We stood on either side of the sawdust-stomping horse, each holding one cheek strap of the frayed halter, our faces separated only by the animal's nervously nodding head making the shaggy forelock bounce. Just hoping Jay's fingers would accidentally bump against mine was like waiting for lightning to reach down and zap a flagpole. Sweat crawled down my back like ants.

 "What about his feet?" I said.

"They're good. Needs shoes soon. "

"Did you ride him? "

"Of course, you knucklehead, " Jay laughed, "Would I ever bring home one I hadn't tried? "

"Is he named? "

"Nope, you get to do that. Any ideas?"

"Not yet. Which stall is his?"

"The box at the far end. I gotta go, take over." He dropped the coiled lead shank into my hand. Off he went to the tack room. The right back pocket of his jeans bloomed with a wallet-shaped fade. I made myself look away.

"Come on, horse, let's go. I just cleaned your room! Fresh shavings, cool water in your bucket, sweet feed in the bin." Just kept talking low and calm to give him confidence. I might even convince myself.

In a week I named him. *Golden Ruler.* Every morning when I finished mucking out the stalls, feeding and watering Jay's horses, I turned Ruler out to stretch and roll in the paddock, then curried his coat to yellow satin.

"If I treat you right, Ruler, " I told him, sharing a carrot or apple, "you'll be good for me too." He flared his velvet nostrils, bumped my shoulder with his muzzle. Proudly, I burned his name into a wooden plaque to tack over his stall, and ordered a brass strip to buckle on the brow band of his leather hackamore.

Jay made me work Ruler relentlessly, one hour every morning, two hours every afternoon. We practiced in the indoor arena; we worked in the paddock behind the barns.

"I want you to set an example to my new riders," Jay said. "Show them how it's done."

"You mean, show them what a good teacher their "Mr. G." is?"

He insisted all his students, no matter what age, call him that. I only called him Jay in my fantasies or when we were alone, polishing tack.

Was I teasing him? Of course. Did it matter? Not a bit. He just grinned and scuffed away, arrogant as ever.

I wanted to be out on the trail and explore, but Jay insisted I learn to jump up bareback, take Ruler through all his gaits and leads, pause, reverse, back up, drop the reins and stop with just a shift of balance or slight pressure to the withers. It was both boring and challenging, repetitive and different. Never mind that Ruler had moods or I had sore muscles. I would be the best student Mr. G. had ever had. I would show off. I would not be frightened. I would work harder than anyone.

By September, I had watched, learned and practiced, and evidently passed some unwritten test of Jay's, because Ruler and I finally were allowed to ride on the trail on our own.

Late one Sunday, we jogged across the street, under the highway bridge, through the forest preserve toward Long Pond. Once, Ruler shied at blowing newspapers, but I did not fall off; he pranced and cantered, and came to a sudden stop, but I stayed on. No saddle, no bit in his mouth, just the two of us, communicating (as Jay would say, "Check the flip of his ears, watch for the shiver of his hide, feel his muscles between your legs, COMMUNICATE with your animal"). Cloud shadows chilled my shoulders. My ankles, knees and hips embraced the rhythmic thudding of Ruler's hooves on the packed earth of the trail.

Then, around a bend, a storm-downed tree blocked our path, branches and leaves flapping. Ruler skidded to a snorting halt, balked, backed up, whirled, faced it again.

I clutched his mane with one hand, reached forward for the headstall of his hackamore, settled my knees deep into his shoulders, squeezed his withers. He had never been trained to jump. Could he go over? Could I stay on if he did? Should we go back? He half reared and whirled again. No way to go around, roots and brambles on one side, branches and rocks on the other. Why wasn't that damn Jay here to tell me what to do?

Out loud to the wind, to my horse, to myself I chanted, "Hey, I'm a grownup. Grownups do hard things. This is hard. I can do this. I can do this!"

The tree trunk was only knee high when I prodded Ruler up close to measure it. He backed up, took a loping start, coiled, sprang over with front legs tucked, his head and my hands reaching forward, then we thumped down together, graceful as Pegasus, easy as a seesaw.

No one was there to see us, but for once I did not care. Would Jay believe me if I told him later? Maybe, maybe not. I had never jumped with a horse before and I never did again. It was our own moment, mine and Golden Ruler's, and that was all that mattered.

Bobbi's articles and poems have been published in the regional publications *Here in Hanover* and *Kearsarge Magazine.* Her favorite authors include: Robert Frost, Rudyard Kipling, A.A. Milne, and Maxine Kumin.

Invitation to Play

The Prompt:

This was not an in-class exercise, but a homework assignment (I don't usually give homework, but the class insisted!). I read a brief description of a riverbank and asked each to imagine a character standing on that riverbank, thinking about something he or she had lost. Bobbi's response:

Delilah

This was her favorite jumping in spot, right here on the high edge of the bank where the river shouldered its way beneath, slowing the current, creating an undercut. Muskrats and beavers sliding here have worn the grass smooth as hair gel. Delilah always paused, sniffed the tracks, then the air, then plunged in, head high, paws swimming even before they hit water. Her tail, a black silk rudder, left a trailing V.

And how she loved to swim. I'd twirl the frayed rope of the canvas dummy and she'd head right to its splash spot, the webs in her front feet splayed out giving her speed and pull like the flippers I used to wear when I was still young enough to snorkel. Forty, fifty times I'd throw, she'd retrieve. After a few good shakes, she'd roll in the grass, then stretch out next to me, blinking her eyes slow, slower as the sun warmed her.

In summer, water beaded up on her back as she swam; it only took two shakes for the top coat to dry. In winter, when she loped out onto shore, her double coat turned crisp with ice. Even her whiskers and eyelashes were decorated.

"Are you my frosted mini-wheat?" I'd say. Her black lips smiled, her pink tongue licked my gloves as I rubbed her neck and back dry.

That first summer when she was still a pup and I could still get up off the ground okay, I'd jump in and swim with her, float a ways down the river, and feel the water hold me up like wide, warm hands. We let the slow current take us around the bend to the sandy spot where folks often launch canoes or kayaks. The water was cleaner in those days, smooth, quietly nudging its way around roots and rocks.

Delilah was fearless then, and I wasn't so afraid of tripping and falling. Wherever I went, she'd go, bumping her black nose on my leg as we rambled the paths leading to the river. We could hear it better then, too, especially after a good rain, the thrash of it against rocks, the slap of it on the shore edge. We came here every day at sunrise, to watch a moose crash through shrubbery, or for a swim, or just to breathe in forest smells. When she was a year old, her head finally came to the perfect spot by my knee where my hand could stroke the taffeta of her ears. I loved the smell of her wet fur drying in the sun or the sweet rawhide scent of her panting when we finally drove home. For fourteen years, we were always together, she was always there for me, with me. We didn't walk as fast as we used to, our breathing was slower, sometimes we moaned in our sleep.

Then came last month. We had both started to limp at about the same time. My doc said I could have a hip replacement. But Delilah's vet said the lump on her shoulder was bone cancer. She grunted with each step. She could no longer jump into the front seat of the truck. She would never chase the pink ball again. In the mornings, she began to look up at me from her foam bed in the living room, thump her tail softly, then sigh and swim back down into her sleep.

~ ~ ~

So, on this dismal March afternoon, I have brought her fragments back here to the edge of our river. How is it that 90 pounds of bone, sinew, whiskers, and love have become mere confetti, shiny as mica, crammed into this coffee can? Every particle of her, cupped in my hands. Cold wind that smells like rain on marsh grass and the inky water below me must carry her away.

The river is noisy now, chuckling around pebbles and twigs and chunks of logs. River, how dare you laugh?

She was always just here, here with me and beside me, and now she's just not. Oh, beloved Delilah, go...let the current swirl all those little bits of you away. The real you is pain-free at last, free to go galloping on those heavenly green fields with all your former buddies and human pals. Watch for me, it won't be long; I'll see you soon.

Previously published in Kearsarge Magazine.

The Prompt:

The writing process is different for each person. There is no wrong or right way to be creative. I asked each writer to envision her writing process, and to write a metaphor to illustrate that idea. Bobbi's response:

Metaphor

I undo the ribbon of a velvet bag of marbles of hand-blown glass, letting them roll as they will. Some are large and streaked, red banners of blood floating in clear rain-glass. The blue ones, cobalt as yesterday's sky, being easier to sort, click like-to-like—they herd and huddle together. I flick the marbles out to separate, watch the little ones, the banana yellow ones, scamper across crevices in the carpet, becoming tucked and stuck in the cut pile of indecision. My favorite, the only purple one, has a chip, a nick that causes it to wobble and waver not knowing where to settle...trying this phrase, that emotion, until finally, channeled in the crack of the pine floor where planks join—a wooden sluice or groove that leads to a knothole—the safety of a cupped palm, where it can nestle...then I begin to write.

The Prompt:

This prompt, another rare homework assignment, is designed to illustrate how a writer might decide which point of view works best for a particular piece. Writers were instructed to develop a story in the first person. Bobbi's response:

The Tapestry

Something made the tapestry move slightly, just a quiver, no more than a breath or the wiggle of a mouse scampering behind it. The tapestry, nearly 20 feet tall, hangs from ceiling to floor in my Grandma's house in Boston. The scene shows Daniel subduing a lion by pulling its head backwards. I pass the hanging every time I go up to my own bedroom.

There is a sudden shiver on the tapestry's purple velvet edge from the top of the stairs, as I head up after supper. Grandma and I had shared a simple meal together in the dim first floor dining room on whose walls hung twelve animal heads; bear, elk, deer, and moose stared down with marbled eyes. Does Daniel's lion know it might be the next to hang there?

Grandma likes to stay on to finish her café au lait and peach melba while Delia, her maid, carries dishes to the dumbwaiter in the pantry. No one else is home in Grandma's five-story brownstone. The hallways echo with emptiness and shadows. But I have homework to finish, plus a test tomorrow in my most annoying class—algebra. No time for ghosts, or poltergeists, or whatever gremlin lurks behind the scene of *Daniel and the Lion*. If only the colors of the lion's wind-blown mane, wet tongue, and teeth weren't so realistic. If only whoever had plied the needle in and out of those tiny squares to create the scene had been less talented, less realistic. As he wrenches open the lion's jaw, Daniel's bearded face grimaces right at my eye level. I turn my head away so nightmares of the lion's roaring and Daniel's grunting won't haunt me.

One more step, one more, and I'll be past. But it moves again, a slight billowing like a fat man's belly, inflating then deflating with a rush of warm, stale air smelling of mothballs like Grandfather's morning breath before he puts in his dentures.

I have to reach behind the tapestry to turn on the light switch so I can see up the rest of the stairway. My room is safely down the hall beyond, but will I make it? If only my parents were home, I'd feel safer. If I touch the tapestry, will it stop quivering? Or, will the lion's head become real, and reach for me with its shiny spit-slick fangs? Or, will Daniel drop the club raised over his shoulder and grab my hair instead of the lion's mane? One more step, just one more. Just do it, I tell myself, just go on by, it's only colored threads and burlap.

Jut then the coal furnace in the cellar chugs and groans to life, and a sudden gust of hot breath swells the tapestry, wrapping it around my ankles. The lion bellows; Daniel roars with laughter at my terror.

The Prompt:

The second part of the point of view assignment was to write the same story in the third person. Bobbi's response:

The Tapestry (from the maid's point of view)

Her feather duster flickered soundlessly here and there up the stairs, caressing newel posts, tickling banisters. If only her knees didn't click and crackle so loudly, no one would know she was approaching. Soon she'd smear more liniment on the parts that ached the most. Ah, but then the smell would give her away. She'd finished the dining room, the front hall, and every knick-knack in the gold parlor without knocking a single one of them over. The Old Missus ought to be pleased this time.

"Delia," Old Missus called out, "Oh, Delia dear, don't forget to sweep the cobwebs from the tapestry with that little broom of yours as you go by. Thank you!"

Old Missus had a soft, quivery voice nowadays, but if she got angry at a job done only part way, her voice cut sharp as winter wind. Delia patted the little whiskbroom in her apron pocket. Good, she'd do that job fast and well.

"No, M'am, I won't forget."

That huge wall hanging had been there forever guarding the stairs to the third floor, gathering generations of cobwebs and mouse dust in its fringes and along its burlap backing. She hated how a sudden draft could make its heavy fabric flap and jitter, and make the half-naked man with hair to his shoulders wiggle. Even the lion shivered as if it was really alive and would finally jump out of its threads and stitches to grab her with its white, wet teeth. Why anyone would hang such an enormous thing on a wall in their house was beyond her. Supposed to keep cold drafts away, so Anna the cook had said. But why not just stoke the furnace a bit?

"Don't you try and kill me this day." She shook the duster at the lion, smacking feathers on its bleeding snout. Its yellow eyes squinted, the whiskers twitched, the tapestry breathed, pulling away from its wall then sucking back in tightly against it.

"Don't you dare snarl at me, or one of these days I'll just ravel out every one of your threads and you'll be nothing but a tangled mess of yellow and brown yarns on this stair runner!"

Delia rap-rap-rapped her short cobweb broom as high up on the tapestry as she could reach, then scurried to the safety of the third floor where Young Missus slept.

THESAURUS ENTRY: **determine**
PART OF SPEECH: *verb*
DEFINITION: discover, decide
SYNONYMS: figure out, learn, hear, see, check, detect, unearth, purpose, invent, shape, plot

MAKING CONNECTIONS

My love of stories began early. My father would sing to me at bedtime, and the stories from those songs painted pictures of people in trouble, of faraway places, of beauty in the ordinary. I would wake up to my mother singing show tunes, which also fueled my imagination. With a happy childhood spent largely out-of-doors, followed by years of discovery, my many interests and experiences are a good draw for a writing life.

I love fiction because it allows me to find the adventures I crave; I can be anyone, go anywhere, solve problems, and live the lives of my characters. I believe there is more truth in fiction than most people realize. Take a bit of real life, combine it with imagination, and there you have it, a new, original tale. One of my favorite quotes is, "Be careful or you'll end up in my novel!"

I met Deb McKew at a school function, and quickly realized her classes were for me. The group magic that happens weekly is a lifeline for me, and for my writing. To see my work through the eyes of my classmates, to learn to listen, and to be brave in the face of criticism, are all key to improving. Deb's attention to detail, and unwavering support of my writing, has encouraged me to keep at it even through the roughest of times. The classes spark new ideas on old themes, and the laughter doesn't hurt, either.

Currently, I freelance and write novels. I live in Concord, New Hampshire, and am married to my high school sweetheart. We have two better-than-average children who remind us daily to keep it real.

Deb's Insights:

On the last day of my Tuscany writing retreat, I was sitting at an outdoor café with Sally and her mom overlooking the piazza in Cortona. A wedding party was gathering on the grand steps of the town hall. Sally began recounting facts about the people we were watching: where the bride's family lived ("just up that hill and to the left"); how the aunts were trying to outdo one another with their brightly colored hats ("Look at those two who are walking side by side, they really despise one another."); why the couple opted for a simple weekday ceremony ("They are splurging on a honeymoon in Greece."). I marveled at how she obtained all this information; had she by chance met someone from the party earlier that morning? "Oh, no," she said, "I just made it up."

That is Sally. She has an uncanny ability to create characters and situations out of thin air. To someone with my journalistic sensibilities, that is a wondrous gift. When Sally first joined my workshops, she had already completed the first draft of a young adult novel. She hadn't shown it to anyone; she just wanted to see if she could do it. She admitted that she loved starting new projects, but hated revision. After a few workshops, and helpful feedback from the writing group, Sally realized that maybe she should take her novel out of the drawer and rework it. And so she did. She revised that first novel, has nearly completed her second, and is now working on a third. In between, she's been selling stories to magazines, searching for an agent, and journaling her astute observations in her blog.

Sally works hard to continue improving her writing skills; she comes to every class eager to learn something new. Then she goes home and applies it. She has discovered that the magic is in the revision; what she once resisted, she now embraces with enthusiasm and determination. Her characters are a fun and necessary part of her life, and she revels in her power to control what happens to them.

GRACIE'S GARDEN
(An excerpt of a novel in progress)

The Birth of Gracie's Garden:

Sally: *For several years I had been ruminating on one particular character. She didn't have a name, but she had a life. She believed it was her calling to "rescue" plants from her neighbors' homes, plant them in her yard, and raise them as her own. Some would call this stealing; she knew it to be a moral imperative. When it was my turn to submit work to be critiqued in class, I was at a very sensitive place in the novel I was already working on, and I wasn't ready to share it. Instead, I gave my plant thief a name, Gracie, and a few friends, and dropped them in a setting familiar to me, the town where I grew up. That is how Gracie's Garden was born.*

Deb: *I knew that Sally was just beginning to shape an idea for a new novel. She had her main character, but wasn't quite sure where she was going with her. To help her generate ideas, I used the opening chapter of her draft in a class workshop. Each writer started with one paragraph Sally had written and then continued the story, developing the characters' motives and personalities in their versions.*

Sally: *Deb chose the part in the chapter where Gracie is reading a story about a fig and walnut cake in the food section of the newspaper. The writers in the class were supposed to start with my original words, and then take off in their own directions, using their own imaginations. It was fun to see where everyone went with this colorful character whom I had grown very fond of. The ideas that percolated that day are still with me, and I smile to think of Gracie's alternative universes.*

Chapter 1 – Two Strangers Meet

Wednesday. *Food Section Day.* Peeling back the front-page scandals for more pertinent news, Gracie "tsk, tsked" her dirty fingernails while discovering it was "celebrating figs week." She wondered why anyone would celebrate a fig, but her pen remained steady as she wrote her shopping list. With the last sip of Red Rose tea, Gracie folded up the *Weymouth News*, then stood to stretch her sore back.

Just then, she heard Rambler scratch at the door. Opening the peeling wooden door to let him in, Gracie reveled in the scent of her latest prize, a Miss Canada lilac. "It was a banner day yesterday, old boy. Can you smell that?" Rambler yowled his affirmation. "Good boy." Gracie scuffed over to the treat jar to toss her pet a biscuit.

"Almost time for our walk, Ram." Rambler's head cocked to one side at the word "walk." Gracie rubbed her fingertips with her thumbs as she puttered around the house tidying her morning mess. Rambler's tail wagged in earnest anticipation, because she was dressed and tying her shoelaces, the final step before their ritual hour-long walk. Map in one hand, leash in another, and plant diary and pen in her sweater pocket, Gracie set out for the other side of town with her faithful companion. With their noses pointed west, Gracie and Rambler's respective olfactories were in high gear.

While passing the junkyard two doors down from her home, Gracie noticed, among the old cars, trucks, and assorted junk parts, a teenage boy poking around an abandoned tractor-trailer bed.

The teen wasn't aware of the onlookers. He opened the door to the back end of the trailer, stepped inside, and stood still for a moment, allowing his eyes to adjust. With paint-stained palms, he smoothed back his long brown hair. "Yes, this will do. Perfect."

Gracie paused for Rambler, who was intent on a dandelion poking up in the middle of the sidewalk. She wondered about this boy. From 20 yards away, she could tell he was strong by the way he pulled back on the towering, rusting tractor-trailer door. He made easy work of the sliding lock, then propped the door open with a large piece of metal.

She also surmised he was an organized sort by the way he began to assess the contents of the trailer bed; he pushed some things to one side while moving others to the back. He is thoughtful, methodical, mused Gracie, who was enjoying this boy in his natural state, much like the robin building a nest in her backyard.

Gracie enjoyed watching people and animals from a distance. Not realizing he had an audience, this boy was not self-conscious. Gracie took a final look back at the action inside the trailer, then, gently tugging on Rambler's leash, said, "Let's go, boy." Both dog and owner set off again to the West End with hopes of viewing a prize-winning garden.

Pulling her worn leather diary out of her pocket, Gracie looked down at the carefully lettered address while whispering to her dog, "Okay, Ram, almost there. 101 Bellevue Avenue. The article said this won the South Shore landscape architects' grand prize last year. We may actually see the iris we've been looking for. It should be almost ready to transplant." Rambler responded by keeping his attention on the smells of this part of town, as if he was helping discover the new find.

Turning the corner from West Main to Bellevue, Gracie smelled it before she could see it: a garden designed for a young couple by an expensive landscape architect from Boston. Then she saw it. The garden at 101 Bellevue reminded Gracie of a woman she had seen in church the previous Sunday, resplendent in her colorful June jacket and summer perfume. Pink Cape Cod roses spilled over a white fence, magenta dianthus nestled themselves into a small rock garden, blue bachelor buttons flopped this way and that, ribbon grass reached for the sky. Heavy with their top-weight and supported by stakes, elegant, soft white peonies sent their perfume to the rest of the garden, as if to remind all how special they were. Thankfully, at the edge of the yard, Gracie spied three huge clumps of tall blue bearded iris, majestic and commanding, and almost gone by.

Tears filled Gracie's eyes as her thumbs went to work on her fingertips. She could feel the loose mix of compost and rich dark soil anchoring the beautiful iris. She could taste the just-right acid in the soil. Most of all, she could see these dark blue beauties clumped up next to her soon-to-be rock garden filled with sedums from the blue-ribbon winning Richelsons' yard over on Eaton Hill. Rambler was getting anxious; Gracie's mumbling and twitching caused the dog to whine and circle, alerting his mistress to his presence. "It's okay, boy, let's go."

On her way home, Gracie scoped out a parking spot close to the iris but far enough away from streetlights. In a now-perfected routine, she figured out the best route to and from her home on North Street. She'd read in the paper that it would be overcast that night, so Gracie figured she'd better take advantage and rescue her iris while conditions were perfect. Besides, the plant was ripe for transplant; any later in the summer and there might be problems.

As they approached their own neighborhood, Gracie glanced down the junkyard slope once more and noted that the boy was still rearranging the back of the trailer. Rambler and Gracie stopped to watch.

With his back to the pair standing on the sidewalk, Dalton assessed the quality of light, debating where to put the Formica table upon which he would eventually place his art supplies. When he reached out his right hand to move the table, he felt something slice through the outer edge of his hand. "Shit," he seethed, watching a rivulet of red trickling from his finger to his wrist. Scrambling around for something clean to wipe his hand, Dalton turned toward the open door and the street. He blinked in the bright sunlight, just catching a blur of pink approaching him. He squeezed his wrist, holding his hand above his head, waiting for his eyes to adjust. A grinning little grey-haired, lady, all in pink, and her scruffy white dog were staring at him.

Watching the boy hold up his injured hand, Gracie waved and gingerly made her way down the talus of asphalt to where he was standing. "Can I help you with that?" She pulled a hanky out of her pocket and handed it to Dalton. "I'm Gracie; this is Rambler. We saw you as we were walking by."

"Oh, yeah, uh, thanks." Dalton took the white hanky decorated in pink roses and wrapped it around the palm of his right hand. Bright red blood quickly spread across the cloth, erasing any evidence of the pink roses. "Uh, I'm really sorry. I'll get you another one," he apologized to Gracie, who had been intently staring at the boy's bleeding hand.

"Not a'tall—don't you worry. I have more hankies. Do you live close by? You need to get that cleaned up."

"Not really, I live up by The Rock."

"Well, I live right there," chirped Gracie, pointing to her tiny yellow house. "Come with me and I'll get you my first aid kit. You can clean up in my bathroom." Not sure what else he could do, Dalton followed Gracie and Rambler home.

Chapter 2 – Color and Light

As far back as Dalton could remember, he'd sorted the world into colors. Looking around Gracie's kitchen, he felt oddly comfortable, enveloped in the entire spectrum. From where he sat, Dalton noticed blue and yellow wallpaper with pink and green flowers, a red teakettle, black and white kitty cats who sprinkled salt or pepper, purple oven mitts, an orange leather-bound book, and directly in front of him, a tablecloth with watermelons surrounded by green lime slices.

The room smelled like apples, cinnamon, and dog. Dalton's newly gauzed hand throbbed. While Gracie heated a pan of chicken noodle soup, Rambler stood beside Dalton, panting for attention. "He likes you." Dalton scratched Rambler's ears until the mutt settled down. "What's your name?"

"Oh, sorry, I'm Dalton, Dalton Spoon."

While pouring the entire pan of soup into a giant blue bowl, Gracie asked, "Now Dalton, what's so interesting in that old trailer?"

Dalton looked down at the piece of paper in front of him. The words, *fig and walnut coffee cake ingredients*, written in a flowing, purple script, were followed by a long shopping list. "Oh, well, I need some space. It doesn't look like anyone's using it right now, but there's some furniture back there. Is anyone living there?"

"Why? Do you want to live there?"

"No, I want to work there. I paint."

"Well, well, a painter. Lovely. What exactly do you paint, Dalton?" Gracie asked as she placed the bright blue soup bowl in front of this stranger in her kitchen.

"Thanks." Dalton slurped several spoonfuls, and then rested. "Until recently, graffiti. Right now, I'm in a dark period. I'm reading a lot of seriously dark fiction and poetry, and I'm painting what I read." He glanced up at the painted tin light fixture hanging just above him. "I want to work on this motel room murder I'm reading about—really dark, you know?"

"No, I really don't, but it sounds interesting, Dalton. Why do you want to paint a murder scene in the junkyard?"

Dalton picked up the bowl to drink the rest of the broth, then thought better of it; he put the bowl back down on the table. "I don't know," he shrugged. "I guess I want to be by myself, with no distractions. When I painted graffiti, I always did it in the middle of the night."

"Well, you might be alone, but you might not. Kids come and go in the junkyard. I wouldn't leave anything valuable."

"No, I'll take my stuff back and forth with me." Dalton stood to bring his bowl over to the sink. "Thanks for the soup. The first aid, too." He held up his bandaged appendage and continued, "I gotta get going."

"Hold on." Gracie held up her hand in traffic-cop fashion. "I don't get a lot of visitors, especially teenagers. I've a favor to ask."

"Sure," Dalton agreed, without knowing the favor.

"Out back, follow me." With Rambler at her heel, Gracie gave Dalton a quick tour of her "prize-winning" garden. As they followed a set of cobble pavers that wound around azaleas, hydrangeas, lilies, and various grasses, Dalton was awestruck by the layers of color and light in Gracie's backyard. He had never seen a space quite like this. Little blue flowers with pointed petals gave way to taller purple fuzzy flowers and still taller yellow and white fluffy beauties that looked good enough to eat. In between were more shades of green than Dalton had in his paint box. They arrived at a small sturdy wooden bench, where Gracie sat while Rambler went off in search of chipmunks.

Standing at the back of Gracie's property, Dalton scanned the yard. "This is one beautiful garden, Gracie. Did you do all this yourself?"

"You betcha—Rambler and I are out here every day. See the bush by the back door?" From where Gracie was sitting, there was a perfect view to the Miss Canada. "That lilac was planted yesterday; looks like it's always been there, doesn't it?" she continued, almost as if she were talking to herself. "Probably shouldn't have transplanted at this time, but it is cool enough. I just had to have the scent here in the garden before all the blooms go by." Dalton noticed Gracie rubbing her thumbs and fingers in a most peculiar way, almost like she was feeling the dirt sift through her fingers.

145

"Did you need me to do something back here?" Dalton asked, hoping to snap Gracie out of her trance.

"Oh, my, yes. Thank you. I get so distracted in my garden." Pointing to a small three-sided potting shed, Gracie said, "Go get my nursery spade, the yellow one." When Dalton returned with the shovel, Gracie stood over a worn-out bed of tulips. She went around the aged flowerbed with the shovel, marking the perimeter. "There. If you could dig up this space and loosen the dirt to about eight inches deep, that would be marvelous."

They had both forgotten about Dalton's wounded hand. As he began to dig, he winced, but kept the pain to himself. "What's going in here next?"

A wide grin lit Gracie's face; even her eyes smiled. "It's a secret. You can come back Friday and see for yourself."

Smoothing his chestnut hair out of his eyes, Dalton said, "Okay then, I'll be back Friday." He had been secretly hoping to come back just to get the colors straight in his mind. "Do you mind if I bring my paints?"

Still beaming, Gracie clapped her hands together once. "Absolutely, bring your paints."

Chapter 3 – Seeing for the First Time

All the way home, Dalton thought about Gracie's garden, wondering how to conjure up just the right blue and capture that perfect yellow, which towered above all the other flowers. Tapping his left hand on his thigh to an internal rhythm, Dalton remembered a specific day when he had fallen in love with yellow. He was next door, at Mrs. Cleary's house.

Dalton used a paintbrush long before pencil or pen. When only 3 years old, he began spending time at his neighbor's house, while his parents both worked; this daily routine lasted for several years.

During his first visit, Mrs. Cleary gave Dalton a paintbrush, jars of finger paints, and butcher paper. At first, he painted with his fingers as any young child might, but then something stirred within him, like a katabatic wind to a mountaintop perpetually shrouded in fog. The winds of change were swift to Dalton's young mind, and he returned again and again to stay with Mrs. Cleary, who kept baskets of toys for her grandchildren, but art supplies for Dalton.

He was barely 5 years old when, one day, Mrs. Cleary brought out several tubes of acrylic paint along with new paintbrushes. They were perfect the way they all lined up in a white plastic tray; each tube had a color strip across its middle that indicated the color inside. Dalton stared at them. "Go ahead, honey, these are for you," said his caretaker, who had recognized his tactile nature as well as his affinity for painting.

The boy remained silent, running his fingers back and forth across the slippery paint tubes while absorbing the colors in his head. The tubes were cool to his touch, but his mind was on fire. He couldn't read yet, so the word cadmium meant nothing to him, but that bright, happy ray of color captured the 5-year-old's imagination. Thinking about all the things he could paint with those colors, especially the yellow, he quickly realized that those paints were far prettier than any he had been using. Dalton never used cheap toy-store paints again.

Now, passing Mrs. Cleary's house on his way home, Dalton thought about his time there, and wondered how long it would have taken him to discover painting if it weren't for the old lady. When he entered elementary school, he stopped going next door; he was old enough to be home alone, finish his homework, and get a snack until one of his parents arrived. He barely saw Mrs. Cleary after that, and then she moved away to her son's house somewhere out West. A new family lived there now.

As he approached home, he saw his father's car in the driveway. Dalton, thinking back to the previous night when he'd had a terrible fight with his father, tried to sneak in the back door in order to escape to the cellar, where his room and art supplies were, but his old man happened to be in the kitchen. Confrontation was unavoidable.

The smell of old beer and new bourbon greeted Dalton. "Hi, Dad."

With a loll of his head, Jim Spoon looked up at his only child. "Hey, buddy. Where you been?"

"Just out, Dad, like always."

"Why you always going out?" slurred Dalton's father, wiping drool off his chin. "What's wrong with being home sweet home?"

"Nothing, Dad," said Dalton, seeing his kitchen for perhaps the first time in his life. Everything was dingy grays and browns: dishes stacked high in the sink; curtains from another decade; a floor so thick with dirt that the once diamond-shaped impressions of the linoleum were no longer visible. No watermelon tablecloth, no purple oven mitts, no cute kitty-cat salt shakers. "I thought you were supposed to be at work today."

"Oh, well, you know, some days they need me, some days they don't. I hung out at Barney's to see some of the guys on their lunch hour."

"I can tell." Luckily for Dalton, his father didn't bring up, or possibly even remember, their most recent argument, so he could spend the rest of the afternoon painting. "I'll be downstairs." Dalton tromped down the steps, leaving his old man to figure out just what it was he wanted to talk to his son about.

Laying out a large piece of cardboard that he had retrieved from the dumpster at the mattress supply house down the street, Dalton prepared his palette by squeezing the cadmium yellow and cerulean blue. His thoughts turned to the previous night.

It wasn't unusual for Dalton to come home late, so he was surprised to see his father awake and waiting for him, the glow of the television inviting him into the living room. "Hey, Dad, what's up? Kinda late, isn't it?"

"Exactly what I was thinking," said Jim Spoon. A bottle of Budweiser dropped from his hand, rolled across the floor, and came to rest at Dalton's feet. "You're never home anymore. What the hell do you do all day and night?"

Taking a seat on the couch opposite his father, Dalton chose not to be intimidated by his father's drunken state. "Well, I work four mornings a week, all weekend long too, then I just hang around, you know Dad, just hang out. It's summer. What's the problem?"

"The problem is that John Arnold said he saw you with a group of kids at the cemetery the other night—drinking and raising hell!"

"So? I wasn't breaking any laws. No big deal."

Jim Spoon picked up an empty bottle and threw it at the wall beside Dalton. It landed with a thud on the carpet next to his son's leg. "No big deal?! You were breaking about three laws, and it is a big deal if John Arnold is complaining. He owns Labor Ready; I need that job. Keep your nose clean. No more drinking in the cemetery near Arnold's house. Now, go get me another beer."

Dalton didn't even blink. "Looks like you've had enough."

"What? You little shit, get me a beer. Now." Jim Spoon leaned over the side of his chair to pick up another stray beer bottle. While still bent over, he grabbed the bottle and side-armed it at Dalton's head. Dalton ducked, but it was a close call.

"What the fuck is the matter with you?" Dalton had shouted. He marched to the fridge, grabbed as many bottles as he could manage, then rushed at his old man and unceremoniously dumped them all in his father's lap. "Is this enough? How many is enough, Dad?" Dalton then stormed off to his room. Jim Spoon was left with a pile of beer bottles on his lap and a pained expression across his face.

"Same shit, different day," mumbled Dalton as he now focused back on his work in the basement. Grabbing an oversized house-painting brush, Dalton dug into the gesso white and jammed the paint onto the cardboard. His father had always been a beer drinker, but only occasionally had Dalton seen him falling-down drunk—until lately. Something was up; things were getting worse.

While he waited for the gesso to dry, Dalton turned up the radio, loud. With the sound of his favorite music beating out an earthy rhythm, Dalton blended a perfect mix of yellow and blue to get the base green down for a portrait of Gracie's garden. He wondered if his father was angry at his mother, or if it was something else. The two of them had always managed to dance around the subject of "the big leaving," which was how Dalton referred to his mother's abandonment.

Dipping into the fresh green paint, Dalton made wide strokes, working all of the muscles on the left side of his body. He nearly completed the background in less than 15 minutes. His right hand was still throbbing, so Dalton put on his head phones to distract him from the pain. With the pulsating sounds of the music calming him, he sat back on his bed and stared at the background layer of the garden painting. It shimmered under the fluorescent lights. He thought that natural light would be much better and decided to finish the piece at Gracie's.

Staring into space, Dalton played "what if?" What if she was really sick, he thought, and the only doctor was in California? She doesn't want to upset us, he reasoned, so when she gets better, she will be back, all healthy and ready to live as we used to live.

He fell asleep with these thoughts on his mind. He dreamed about colors. And his mother. She was wearing a faded pink skirt and a graying yellow top. She was trying to tell Dalton something. He could feel it. What was she trying to say? It was always like this; everything about his mother was in the grey zone, just beyond reach. He never really knew what she looked like, what she intended for him, why she left. Nothing was clear. He felt it was his job to make things clear; how to go about it was always the question.

When the music changed to talk radio, Dalton woke suddenly. With a scowl and a headache, he went to work on an old murder scene, which needed a touch of red.

Chapter 4 – Just Some Lady and Her Dog

Thursday. *Travel Section Day.* Gracie had no interest in Greece or the Galapagos, so she lingered over the local section. It caught her eye as soon as she turned the page. Anything about plants, gardens, and flowers usually jumped right off the page for Gracie. The headline read:

PRIZE WINNING SHRUB MISSING

Gracie's fingers started to twitch as she read the article.

Missing: one prize lilac, aka, Lilac Syringa x prestoniae. Approximately four feet tall, three feet wide, bright pink blooms and lovely dark green foliage. Last seen at 1482 Westbourne Street, Weymouth. The owners, Nancy and Paul Thirstenwald, first noticed their prize lilac missing yesterday. "We aren't sure how long it has been missing, we only go out to the garden on weekends, but our gardener alerted us to this just yesterday," said Mrs. Thirstenwald, who appeared quite shaken by the incident.

The article went on to tell a tale of woe from the Thirstenwalds' perspective, but Gracie couldn't take any more. "My goodness, Rambler, they only go out to their garden on weekends? What kind of people are these Thirstenwalds? They don't deserve a prize-winning anything." With a sharp slap to the table edge, Gracie got up and paced about her kitchen. Rambler began to whine, and followed his mistress in circles.

"It's okay, Ram. We'll go about our day as planned. I'll put this fig cake together, then we'll have our walk. But let's stay away from the West End today. Let's go down to the waterfront to see who's about, shall we?" Trying desperately to read Gracie's mood, Rambler finally chimed in his yowl of affirmation and went to his bed to await further instructions, hoping she would drop something yummy.

Mixing her cake, Gracie said, "Hey, Ram, I think we will serve this to that nice young man tomorrow. You know, Dalton, the painter." Rambler panted when Gracie waved the dough-covered spatula at him. "Also, I think I'll ask him to move the stones for the new path." At this, a dollop of dough went sailing over the back of a chair and landed within neck-stretching distance of Rambler. One quick lick and no more dollop. "Good boy!"

After adding the figs, which had been soaking in a bowl of hot water, Gracie popped her cake into the preheated oven, announcing, "I'm going to clean up to get ready for our walk, Ram. We leave in 45 minutes." Rambler stood panting at the promise of a walk.

When she went upstairs to wash, Gracie glanced in the mirror at her 65-year-old self, and became entranced. Her heart slowed, and she stared at the stranger in the reflection. It was a comfortable stare; she couldn't turn away. She was intrigued by the youthful, short-cropped grey hair, and bright blue eyes as round as nickels. The soft folds around her eyes and mouth looked foreign to Gracie. "Where's Grace from Sterling?" she wondered. Her fingers started their rubbing motion as a picture of a Victorian house, painted in amber, gold, and milk chocolate, fleetingly crossed her mind. Autumn leaves sprinkled downward, as laughter echoed from the past and a hint of a smile came to Gracie's lips. With a slow, deep breath, Gracie dragged herself back to the present, and finished cleaning up for her day.

As was her routine, Gracie lay on the floor and stretched her back. The prior evening's activity, digging up the huge clump of iris, had taken its toll. When Rambler, who had come upstairs to look for his mistress, saw that she was on the floor next to her bed, he commando-crawled closer to watch. "I'm sore, Ram." And for the third time that day, Gracie rubbed the lump in her armpit, which she had found only days before, and mentally measured its growth. It seemed to have grown from a peach pit to a small plum since last week. Continuing her chat with Rambler so as not to upset him, Gracie said, "Those irises were a challenge. They were badly in need of dividing. Well, I took care of that, didn't I?" Choosing not to worry, Gracie rolled over, pulled her knees up to her middle in a fetal position, and made one final stretch before she rose to get dressed.

When she stood, another picture from her past popped into her brain. She saw her cousin, in Worcester, who was having her second child. Gracie was staying at her cousin's house overnight to help with the older child, a girl who was 4 years old at the time. It was a Saturday, and she planned to be there until the following afternoon. Gracie shook her head as if there were bees buzzing around. "Let's get that cake out of the oven and get going, Ram."

Putting the newspaper article out of her mind, Gracie led Rambler toward the waterfront and the shipyard. The salt air was strong with an onshore breeze calling Gracie to the Fore River. When they passed the shipyard, she noticed Ed Harrison pulling his skiff up to the rocks next to one of the bridge abutments. They stopped to watch, and Gracie waved when Ed acknowledged them. "Hi, Gracie. Hi, Ram. Out for your morning walk?"

"You betcha, Ed. What's new?"

Ed walked up the boat ramp, bending down to squeeze Rambler's ears. "Not much new, Gracie. But I did catch some flounder. You want a couple for dinner?"

"Absolutely! What a treat."

"Great." Ed trotted back down the ramp to retrieve the fish, which were strung up in a bucket in his skiff. "I had a banner morning," he shouted. "The little doormats have been burrowing in the sand around the outer pilings where the water eddies back, you know, on the outgoing tide? It was too easy, really."

Gracie clapped her hands in wonder as her friend handed her a string of three small flounder, all bug-eyed and shiny. Rambler, sniffing them, offered a lick to make sure they were indeed dead. Ed was still going on about his conquest. "I used minnows today. The flounder love live bait. Minnows are a sure thing, you know, Gracie?"

"Well, I do now, Ed. Rambler and I are very thankful. Please say hello to Maryanne for me. Tell her I'll stop by Monday for our visit."

"Will do, Gracie. Oh, by the way, she is plotting some fancy meal again, you'll be invited soon...beware!" Ed winked at his long-running joke at his wife's expense. Ed and Gracie were the natives, and Maryanne, a New Yorker, was well, an alien. Gracie and Ed played it up every chance they got.

"I'll do my best to be polite when I don't recognize any of the ingredients!" said Gracie with a wave, and she and Rambler continued up Bridge Street. They passed the Labor Ready storefront, and she noticed several men out front, smoking. There was one man in particular who seemed to be staring at her. "Come on, Ram, let's keep moving."

Jim Spoon was sure he had seen that little lady and that white fuzzy dog before, but he couldn't place them. He found it odd that she was carrying a string of fish. She didn't look like the fishing type, especially dressed in a skirt. Where had he seen them? Then it struck him. He had seen these two on his kitchen table that very morning while he was drinking his coffee.

~ ~ ~

Earlier that day, Dalton had been sketching on scrap paper while eating his breakfast. He was an early riser, mainly from habit, but also because of his job at Swane's Market. This morning, as he had every morning since he could remember, Dalton ate a large bowl of cereal with a banana for breakfast. The cupboards weren't exactly over-stocked, but there was always cereal and milk. It was Thursday morning, and with Gracie still on his mind, Dalton began to pen a sketch of his new acquaintance and her dog. He would sketch on any surface available; often it was junk mail, or the white space of the day's newspaper. He was just finishing the final touches on Rambler's ears when Jim Spoon came in for his first of many cups of coffee.

"Who the hell is that?"

"Just some lady and her dog, Dad."

"Weird."

Dalton stood, carried his bowl to the sink, and left for work. The screen door slammed behind him.

Chapter 5 - A New Path

Friday. *Arts Section Day.* Gracie cooed at the picture of Tony Bennett, who was going to be in Boston that weekend. Remembering another time, with soft sweet music on her record player, Harry holding her in his arms, the two of them dancing in their living room in Sterling, Gracie's eyes puddled, but didn't spill over. She shook off the memory, saying aloud to Rambler, "Almost time for our walk, old boy." With a quick glance back at the paper, she noticed the bold headlines in the local section.

The words jumped off the page:

PRIZE WINNING SHRUB STILL MISSING:
POLICE SET UP HOTLINE TO TRACK DOWN THIEF

Eyes darting back and forth across the page, fingers twitching, Gracie read on:

Paul and Nancy Thirstenwald are offering a reward for any tips that lead to the discovery of the whereabouts of their shrub, missing since sometime last week. With a tearful plea, Mrs. Thirstenwald choked back her loss, "If anybody has any idea where my beloved Miss Canada is, please, please, help us rescue her." The police are asking anyone who may have a lead to call 911-TIPS. The Thirstenwald Foundation has offered a $500 reward for the successful reclamation of their beloved plant.

On a similar note, it has been reported that two clumps of iris and a patch of sedums are missing from the west end neighborhood as well.

"For goodness sakes, Rambler! These Thirsten-hoosies didn't even know their lilac was missing for days; their gosh-darn gardener had to inform them. I think Mrs. Hoosie-whatsie is quite an actress, don't you?" Rambler padded over and rested his chin on Gracie's knee. "Let's just stick close to home today, boy." Her voice, a mix of tenderness and concern, bordered on panic. She stood, and reached for the leash.

Outside, Gracie took a deep breath. From her vantage point on the back stoop she admired her blue bearded iris. The new additions watched over her rock garden like sentinels, protecting the little sedums from any possible surprise attacks. She grinned, knowing these babies were home at last.

Passing the junkyard, Gracie thought of Dalton; she hoped he would be over to visit. Maybe I can finally get some of those pavers moved, she thought. She anticipated enlisting Dalton into some serious labor, perhaps benefiting them both. With a gentle tug on Rambler's leash, Gracie headed around the block, past the brook, then the elementary school, and back toward North Street, and home. When she was about to turn onto her street, Gracie noticed a police officer, in a black and white cruiser, pass slowly by, scanning each house. She quickened her step in order to see him pass her home, and when he did, he barely looked, or slowed down. "Rambler, he wouldn't dare suspect us."

~ ~ ~

With the Arts Section still on her mind, Gracie decided to dig up an old Tony Bennett album and relax in her front room, before her afternoon gardening. She sat in her favorite flower-print stuffed chair, which faced the street, and smiled as Rambler finished circling a nest at her feet. Gracie closed her eyes and soon, her husband was there, as well as her three beautiful children. They were animated, lively, just as they were when last she had seen them: Holly twirling to the music; John, tap-tap-tapping his hands on the floor to the rhythm; little Ginger kicking up her chubby legs from her position in her playpen; and Harry, peering over his newspaper, pretending not to notice any of the ballyhoo sprinkled about him, was taking in every movement, each detail, like the Great Sphinx, knowledgeable and content.

Gracie's happy thoughts of family soon clouded over. Gripping the armrests, she began to feel short of breath, a cold sweat forming at the nape of her neck. Alerted to something amiss, Rambler craned his head back and rested his chin on the seat next to his mistress. Gracie patted his head, and began to breathe easier, while Tony Bennett crooned on.

~ ~ ~

Gracie had escaped despair a long time ago; for the ten years following the loss of her family, it chased her. Despair was slow and long, and grey and cloudy. Her sanity was fragile; it was an ice cube sitting in a sink, slowly draining away its shape until only a small puddle remained, the unrecognized form just waiting for someone to come along and wipe it away without a thought. Once a perky, vibrant woman, she had become a sullen creature heavy with hopelessness, watching the walls push in on her as the floor rose and the ceiling lowered until she was literally boxed in to a place she could not recognize.

Once in a while, Gracie allowed herself to go back, but only to the happy moments, never the awful, horrible memories. Listening to "Because of You," their song, Gracie was back home, in Sterling, more than 30 years ago. She marveled at the ability of music to transport her to a pinpoint in time, transcending all other thought, action, life, and allowing her simple existence in that moment.

Lately, when trying to stay in the present, or focus only on happy memories, her unconscious mind would slip, often when she dreamed. Now, though, the episodes were arriving during times of awake. She was nervous about these intrusions, nervous that despair might win all over again. She remembered the feeling of being boxed in by despair, where there were no windows or doors, where the room of despondency isolated her from oxygen and clear thought... *It was a maze, she remembered now, a maze with no cheese and I was the fooled rat going in circles...despair was the end of the road and I couldn't remember the beginning.*

~ ~ ~

The doorbell rang, snapping Gracie out of her spiral, and giving voice to Rambler, who so infrequently heard the doorbell, wasn't positive what he was barking about. "Shhhsh, Ram! Enough!" Gracie rose slowly, rubbing the lump under her arm, while trying to regain the present. "Okay, coming!" she called, as the bell rang again.

Dalton stood on her front steps, holding a large portfolio and carrying a wooden tool case. "Hi, Gracie, how's it going?"

Still a little muddled, Gracie managed a wan smile, opening the door to allow room for Dalton and his supplies to enter her home. "Come on in, I'm glad you're here."

They were simple words; Dalton took a deep breath and his shoulders relaxed. "Me, too, Gracie. Hi, Ram." As he entered Gracie's front room, the smell of lavender and the sound of old fashioned music were opiates to Dalton. He lowered his supplies to the floor, freeing him to rub Rambler's head and shake his paw.

Remembering her idea to enlist Dalton in some garden chores, Gracie perked up. "Follow me to the kitchen; I have a plan for the afternoon." She led the teenager through the short hallway between the living room and kitchen. "Before we go out back, you have to try my new recipe—my walnut fig cake."

Dalton remembered the shopping list with the fancy handwriting, from the other day. "Sounds great. Thanks."

Smiling now, she reached for the cake, careful not to let Dalton see her dabbing at her eyes with her hanky.

Gracie didn't skimp when she carved out a huge hunk of walnut fig cake, placing the giant wedge on a bright orange plate. Setting it in front of Dalton, with a fork and a large glass of milk, she smiled.

"Thanks, Gracie, this looks amazing. You're a real cook." He swallowed his snack in five piranha–like bites, washing it down with the entire glass of milk.

Gracie marveled, remembering another time when her appetite was healthier. "I need a little help before I let you paint."

"What d'you have in mind?"

"Moving rocks. I want to make a new path that goes in front of my sedums and new iris. Do you have time, I mean, will your parents mind?"

The subject of his parents hadn't come up before today, and Dalton liked it that way. "No, I'm on my own until later tonight—let's move rocks."

~ ~ ~

Out back, Dalton first admired the layers of color; the early afternoon light offered just enough shade to get a good feel for the depth of the garden. He took note next of the curve of the space; he wondered why he didn't notice it before. A memory of middle school popped into his head: he was playing cello, with Robbie Maloney to his right, and Miranda Hofstadter to his left. He was listening to their band leader, "Chops," tell the class that they needed to look as sharp as they sounded for the upcoming performance.

This memory prompted him to look closer at the garden—it was laid out like an orchestra. Directly in front, where the violins and cellos would be, was the new pink-flower bush Gracie was telling him about the other day, the new arrival. It smelled heavy but sweet, like too much candy. Dalton thought instantly of Miranda Hofstadter's shampoo, reminiscent of strawberries and cream. Next, Dalton noticed Gracie had laid out tall grasses to divide the sections of the orchestra. They helped organize the flute from the clarinet section, then again, the clarinet from the horn section. In between were some wilted plants, some new green shoots, and many beautiful flowers. Way out by the percussion section, he noticed unusual trees and bushes. He was visualizing the palette he would use, when Gracie's voice broke his reverie; she summoned Dalton down to the task at hand, the walkway. With one last look at Gracie's garden, anxiousness overcame him, one that could only be quelled by painting.

"You see," Gracie was saying, "My stones march all the way to the back, where my bench sits. But, I want them to sort of meander, over there," Gracie pointed to the right, "where my rock garden is."

Dalton, pensive, tapped his fingers on his thigh, and began to pace down the path. "Seems like a lot of work, and I like this path." He walked to the place where the path bent away from the new rock garden and shot straight for the bench. Hoping to cut his labor short, he suggested, "It wouldn't take many more rocks to go from here, at the bend, to your rock garden, kinda like an off shoot of the main path."

"I like your idea, Dalton, but that would mean a lot more trips to the Fore River. I was hoping to be done with this little project sooner."

"What, you brought all these stones here yourself? You carried them?"

"Oh, my, yes. Rambler and I always try to bring something back with us from our walks." With a wistful faraway look, Gracie continued, "Why, just the other day, we came back with three fresh flounder."

Dalton was beginning to notice that Gracie changed the subject a lot. "Do you care if the stones all match? I mean, I saw a heap of bricks over in the junkyard. They'd be perfect here."

~ ~ ~

Within the hour, Dalton had returned with Gracie's wheelbarrow full of bricks. Gracie directed, while Dalton laid the bricks from the original path to the new rock garden.

"This is sort of like painting, isn't it, Dalton?

Dalton, sweating, was all business. "You bet. These will look great here with all these little green and white things poking up around them. I don't want to ruin them."

"Oh, heavens, Dalton, those are creeping phlox. You couldn't possible damage them. They will retreat momentarily, but they will be back with a vengeance. Little devils, they're going to love the rock garden."

~ ~ ~

It was late afternoon by the time Dalton finally began painting, but he was more than a little pleased with his walkway creation. He decided to leave the time-consuming project, his half-finished acrylic of Gracie's garden that he started at home, for later. Instead, he pulled out his watercolor supplies that he always kept in his big black portfolio. Standing on the back stoop, the garden half circling him, his artist's pad resting on the railing, Dalton made quick work of the hardscape of Gracie's garden.

Gracie observed him from her perch in the kitchen, where she sat to watch squirrels and finches fight over seeds. His head and hands darted with focused, bird-like movement—a synchronized staccato. With the occasional involuntary flick of his neck to free a strand of hair from his eyes, she saw in Dalton a familiar art in motion. Once in a while, a small melody would burst out of her, then she would quiet again, never taking her eyes off the painter. It was as if she was trying to figure out the song Dalton was performing while painting a scene of her garden.

With his grays and browns blended into walkway, bench, and tool shed, Dalton proceeded to dip his brush into the yellow-green paint, and set about dividing the garden into an arc. Once again, his head would rise and lower, his hands would flit back and forth from paint tray to paper, creating what looked to Gracie, sitting just to the side and behind him in her kitchen, rhythm manifested.

About an hour after he began, Dalton stood in Gracie's kitchen, sipping iced tea, watching her admire his completed work. "My, my, Dalton, this is, well, it's just lovely." Gracie, so caught up in the painter and his motions, had forgotten that he was actually creating something.

"It's for you, that is, uh, if you want it." Quickly backpedaling, he added, "It'll be wet for a little while, so it should stay here, anyway."

"I know exactly where I shall hang it," said Gracie, eyes twinkling. "When you come back next time, you will see for yourself the most perfect place for this painting."

~ ~ ~

Dalton seldom parted with his work; on his way home from Gracie's he thought about his picture hanging on one of the walls of her home and imagined, not for the first time, his work displayed in museums around the world. Since the sixth grade, he rarely showed his work to anyone. Dalton worried that people would feel they had a duty to say they liked his work, when they really didn't, as if he were eight years old and had just handed them a crayon-colored picture for their refrigerator. Gracie was different. Why is she so easy to be with, wondered Dalton.

There was the another problem—who would he give a painting to anyway? Definitely not his father. His friends wouldn't get it. He had been thinking of giving one to Marissa, a new girl he was interested in, but which one would he give her? His motel room murder scenes would scare her off. Visualizing Marisa with one of his garden pictures, Dalton smiled to himself.

Approaching his own neighborhood, Dalton thought about his mother. Imagining her living in Italy, Dalton played the "what if" game in his head. What if someone was blackmailing her, and she had no choice but to move to Europe? She's probably waiting for us to rescue her from the Mafia, in Sicily. He knew it was a silly game, but he had been playing it since the first week she went missing. It was important he continue to play this game; his mother needed him to figure out the great mystery of his life.

He and his father never spoke about her anymore. For the first two years, it was a nightly conversation. When Dalton turned 13, his father demanded he stop playing the silly game. It wasn't healthy, Jim Spoon had reasoned. So, Dalton quietly continued to search his imagination for the perfect answer. He just needed to go through each possibility until the right one presented itself, sooner or later.

Jim Spoon had never told Dalton about the letter, the one he hid in his top bureau drawer beneath the socks and tee shirts, the one that held the answer Dalton craved. A letter addressed to Dalton and Jim, both, postmarked three months after Alden Spoon slipped out of her life in Massachusetts and into her new one in Kansas City.

If you would like to read more about *Gracie's Garden*, check out Sally's blog at www.sallylucywrites.com.

Sally's stories have been published in *Kearsarge Magazine, Kid Stuff Magazine, Upper Valley Life,* and *Parenting NH.* Her favorite authors are Mark Helprin and Barbara Kingsolver.

Invitation to Play

The Prompt:

Sally was the first person to register for my very first writing retreat in Italy. She and her mom laughed and ate their way across Tuscany. Oh, yeah, they also wrote some pretty cool stuff. When we visited Siena, one of the most well preserved medieval towns in Italy, famous for its architecture, I instructed writers to find a building that inspired them and to sit and write about it. Here is Sally's response:

Siena

Between the vertical lines of brick and mortar the cathedral squeezes into the landscape. Ascending pilgrims make the trek and pass over footprints of Etruscans, Romans, Florentines, and Sienese.

Michelangelo, Pisano, Bernini can be heard between the flapping wings of pigeons escaping down a sun dappled vicolo with a stolen meal.

A slit of daylight, and a testament to a dark time. The unfinished facade announces restraint, compassion, honor, and love.

Ferocious beasts and Roman gentlemen clear the way against blinding stone in hues of white and pink, green and black.

The stone covets secrets old and new. Secrets from the Paleozoic. Secrets whispered by cutters and boatmen. Secrets revealed by artists and writers, and secrets yet to come. It is the stone that tells the story. It is the stone that reveals the alleluia. It is the stone that fills every crevice large and small in a tiny spot on the map but big in the hearts of the citizens of the world who hold Sienna as a sacred, journeying place.

The Prompt:

Absorb the sensuous vibrancy of the vendors' stalls in the Cortona outdoor market. Choose something that strikes you, then telescope in on the details. Sally's response:

The Cortona Market

There is a greasy carnival smell to the air as customers line up at Paulo's sundry shop on market day. While the din of distant shoppers pours from the food carts around the corner, Paulo lifts the side panels of his truck, revealing his shop, and locks them into their roof position.

Setting out blue plastic buckets, brooms and stacks of paper towels, he is ready to begin another Saturday in the Cortona market.

Paulo's fingers rake away a strand of hair, exposing bright curious eyes. He offers a large grin and a "Buon giorno!" to one of the many women here to do their week's necessities shopping. As one woman picks out soap and shampoo, the other customers wait their turn and gab back and forth, gesturing their hands with each inflection. They are a wall of newly coiffed hair and animal prints. Their tongues roll their R's keeping time with the sounds of pigeons clucking and perched on an ancient tiled roof above their heads.

Paulo's fingers adeptly peck at the adding machine, careful to meet his customer's expectation. She studies the receipt and nods her head, agreeing to the contract which just took place.

Paulo grins and in good humor turns to his next customer, "Buon giorno!"

The Prompt:

Simply write about the color White. *Sally's response:*

White

White is what you see when you're not really looking. It is that which is measured by all else around it. It stands in the background bravely accepting second place to fun reds, vibrant oranges, and sea-calming blues. White is integral in understanding all other colors, just as a mother steps back from her children and lets them shine and take their place in the world. The mother for a time is white. We don't always see what she does. We have to really look sometimes.

THESAURUS ENTRY: optimism

PART OF SPEECH: *noun*

DEFINITION: state of having positive beliefs

SYNONYMS: anticipation, calmness, cheerfulness, enthusiasm, happiness, looking on bright side

Joan Chandler

LAUGH, EAT, WRITE (NOT NECESSARILY IN THAT ORDER)

During 35 years as an elementary school assistant and secretary, I collected enough hilarious quotes, notable student antics, and entertaining assignment errors to fill two milk crates. It seemed natural to think that "someday" I might publish a book of these funny stories.

After retiring, I began attending *Words in Play* creative writing sessions, where I explored a variety of writing genres. Stories from school gradually took a back seat to the creation of poetry and essays. My "temporary" enrollment in a six-week class developed into a perennial membership.

My experience in class has been profound. At each meeting we share the details of our previous week's writing; then we participate in actual writing exercises. These activities forced my reluctant brain to examine unfamiliar and challenging ideas. Such tasks, plus the camaraderie and critical feedback from my fellow students, encouraged me to write every day. I'm no longer intimidated by writing. I feel like Ernestine Hemingway!

My husband Rod and I are lucky to live in the scenic town of Sunapee, New Hampshire. Our two grown children and our grandson live nearby. Presently my hobbies and interests, in addition to writing, include family activities, daily walks, adventures with friends, painting signs, cooking and baking, dining out, fanatically following the Boston Celtics and Red Sox, gardening, singing and listening to music, reading…and even skydiving.

Deb's Insights:

Rummaging through my files recently, I found a collection of newsletters I produced for the local elementary school while my son was making his way through grades K-5. At the time, Joan was the secretary in the principal's office. Anyone going in or out of the building had to check in with her, which gave her an interesting vantage point. For the newsletter, Joan wrote a column we called *Joan's Corner*—she even had her own logo, a caricature one of the parents sketched. The column was eagerly anticipated with each issue.

Years later, when Joan retired from her job at the school, she announced she wanted to write a book. While at the school, she had filled boxes with memorabilia, stories, and drawings of her observations and impressions of the people and events that had passed through those halls of learning for over 35 years. She had enough material for 10 books!

From the moment she joined *Words in Play* she was hooked. Each week, she brings her notebooks filled with her writings and she displays an unusual discipline in tracking her life's trials and tribulations—but to Joan, there really are no tribulations, everything (and I mean everything) that happens in her life is just more fodder for her stories.

Joan is a study in contrast. She has the happiest disposition of anyone I know, and yet her favorite time of year is late fall into winter when everything is gray and gloomy here in New England—she especially loves rainy days. Her submissions for the workshop are usually essays or short stories that revolve around her own humorous experiences with colleagues or family, her love of nature, or her adventures as a retiree, all mostly in a narrative format. Her writing exercises in class, however, are starkly different; for one thing, they are usually fictional, deep, dark and always full of vivid sensory detail. After a few workshops, she convinced herself that maybe she should write a novel, but we're still waiting.

Joan truly utilizes the benefits of the writing workshops to her advantage. She will bring in a list, or a thought, or a school anecdote and it will turn into a children's story or a newspaper article. She uses the writing group as a sounding board for her many ideas. She's the one who actually proposed the idea for this book, and we are all grateful for that. I can't imagine not being in Joan's corner…

November

The heavy sky had darkened,
Its brooding clouds hung low
As if they, too, had harkened
To geese who flew below.
Autumnal winds blew through me
With penetrating chill,
Pummeled me and drew me,
Attacked me thus, until
I closed my eyes in rapture,
And, ceasing to resist,
I raised my face to capture
Each wave of biting mist.
Gale winds hit leafless branches
With force to make them crack
While brittle leaves did dances
Against skies cold and black.

I stood with hunched-up shoulders,
Drank in the scene around:
Stark moss and stumps and boulders
Exposed now on bare ground.
Regretting not the rusting
Of autumn's brilliant views,
Instead, completely trusting
In cold November hues,
I thanked whatever reason
Persuaded me to gaze
Upon my favorite season
Of frigid browns and grays.

Previously published in Kearsarge Magazine.

A SHELTERED PLACE

On a sunny day,
When others bask in the heat,
I hunt for that spot in the woods
Where shafts of sun filter down through leaves.
Shelter is easy to find during winter;
The dark is often already there!
A dim light and a wood fire allow me
To hide in plain sight.
I can even disappear inside some music,
So entranced I hear no other sounds.
After a snowstorm
A private room exists under laden pine branches
Where I - unseen - can peek at the white world.
The most profound shelter for me is in the rain.
To lie under a quilt near the open window,
Or sit in a comfy chair near a smudge fire,
Or sit on a wood pile in the dark shed
Provides a haven from the troubles of the world,
But lets me feel these troubles, and be sad.
Safe in that darkened space, I love the sadness.
A hug provides a kind of shelter, too;
Arms can wrap around more than my shoulders.
They enfold my life as it exists in that very moment
As arms, themselves, become a sheltered world.

THE HAVEN

Under the boughs of this balsam exists
A haven, surrounded by snow,
Whose thatched roof will keep away cold, stinging mists
While hiding me safely below.

If I pull on a snowsuit and thick woolen socks
And, properly dressed, crawl inside,
I can peer through a branch at a bunny or fox
Unaware of the room where I hide.

Despite winter's wrath I am cozy and warm,
Made sheltered and safe by a drift;
It is here I curl up to escape from the storm
And savor this rare winter gift.

POURING

A torrent through my veins, the blood is pouring
with life absorbed in all that protoplasm.
It carries spirit and enthusiasm;
While in my head I hear emotions roaring.

Pouring.
Along my face slide rivulets of tears
for families, countries, nations under strife,
for melancholy moments in a life,
for pent-up feelings gathered over years.

Pouring.
Cascades of love pour freely from my heart,
caught in a current, flowing 'til it ends
in willing hearts of family and friends
and others' lives in which mine plays a part.

Pouring.
The cleansing raindrops pound the earth around me,
their noisy drumbeats soothing all my worry,
relieving me of care and stress and hurry,
while nature's remedy for blues has found me.

THE TRAIL

I've wrapped some bracing staples for the day:
a peanut butter sandwich for a snack,
Some cookies to keep hunger pangs at bay,
plus cocoa in a Thermos in my pack.
What thrilling new adventure lies in store?
Snow falls as I anticipate my trek.
My patient walking stick stands near the door
to let me know it wants to leave the deck.
A scarf, a headband, heavy socks (two pairs),
two flannel shirts - my arms can hardly budge;
Thus snugly dressed in warm and wooly layers,
I feel just like a penguin as I trudge.
My face is Vaselined against the breeze
that might soon prove relentless in its sting,
And if the air gets colder by degrees,
the wind's assault will seem less harrowing.
The railroad bed where snowmobilers zoomed
is quiet now, and wide, an easy route.
Someone has kindly motored through and groomed
to make it smooth for snowshoe, ski, or boot.
Right now I'm at the place where, Friday night,
coyotes yipped and howled to celebrate.
On Saturday, we saw signs of a fight –
a deer's leg bone lay in a bloody state.

Like fancy needlework, along the trail,

a thousand turkey tracks march in a line,

Two brown and pale-maize feathers from a tail

adorn a spot beneath a shady pine.

Much smaller stitches decorate the snow;

they merrily meander through brown weeds,

Perhaps a passing partridge (or a crow)

upon its neverending quest for seeds.

An intersection. Which path shall I take?

The straight one leads me through a sheltered wood.

The others, by a farm or to the lake;

I'd strike out on all three roads, if I could!

Gray headstones in the cemetery stand

amid white drifts and under sweeping spruce,

Small branches lie about them close at hand,

where recent wind and ice storms pried them loose.

The mountain looms above the trail's far end,

where it has narrowed to a pencil tip;

Through glasses I can watch as skiers descend,

just dots, careening on a zigzag trip.

Thin charcoal shadows, cast by stems of grass,

are works of art; with such the trail is lined.

Above me, cotton cloud wisps slowly pass.

Tonight I'll miss the trail I've left behind.

METAPHORIA

Waxing poetic about metaphors
Should come to me easy as pie.
I'd personify, maybe use similes,
Be clever, like foxes so sly.
Like steam from a geyser, my words would pour forth;
I'd pen like a Shakespeare or Frost.
As waves on the seashore, descriptions would flow
Like frothy seafoam, tempest-tossed.
Some readers would be so inspired, so psyched,
Their skin would turn red as a beet,
While others, meanwhile, would read eagerly on,
Their rapt faces white as a sheet.
In tune with that rhythmic beat - like a drum,
Their thoughts would be bliss to the core;
While minds once so dull would be sharpened, like tacks,
And opened...much like a door.
With sensory image I'd try to inspire
Each woman, each man, every tyke,
They'd understand after they read it, that I
Never metaphor I didn't like.

Previously published in SooNipi Magazine.

Joan is a regular contributor to the regional publications, *SooNipi Magazine* and *Kearsarge Magazine*. Her favorite authors include John Grisham, Lee Child, Robert B. Parker, and Canadian author Tanya Huff.

Invitation to Play

The Prompt:

Each writer wrote a list of everyday household chores. They then passed the list to the person on their right. Each chose one chore from the new list and wrote using as much sensory detail as possible. (5 minutes) Joan's response (unedited):

Vacuuming

I started with the stairs. The vacuum, set at its strongest power, was like a straw, noisily devouring everything in its path. Bits of carpet fluff, leftover garden soil, lint from black socks - all whooshed like so much propwash through the tube. The occasional paper clip sputtered and clinked, sending little shock waves to my fingers. I saw the discarded pink, lacy underwear too late, and the cleaner let out a high-pitched whine as it tried in vain to suck in the lump of froth. I turned off the machine as it began to emit an odor of burning rayon.

The Prompt:

Write a story using as many "ing" verbs as possible. The goal for the writer is to deliberately overuse phrasing so you can become more aware of it in your writing. Begin your story with the phrase "If I were a magician…" Joan's response (unedited):

If I Were a Magician

If I were a magician, I might be utilizing my talent for many purposes, including: thought-transmitting, allocating major funds to worthy families, communicating with famous dead people, translating foreign languages, and analyzing my friends' psychological problems. Undertaking these assignments would be a way of stimulating my own mind. Developing this craft would require some streamlining of my office, allowing time for producing

and validating ideas, allotting space at my desk, observing the community needs, and packaging the ideas for forwarding to potential customers. I would stay away from conventional magic, including drawing a rabbit out of a hat, sawing a woman in half, retrieving disappearing handkerchiefs, and extricating myself from a suffocating straight jacket while nearly drowning in bubbling water! Were I performing onstage, the audience would be writhing in their seats, marveling at my prowess and enthusiastically applauding.

The Prompt:

The unedited responses to the prompts illustrate the power of the creative mind when the editor inside your head is quiet. You can use any image, but my favorites are those that make you look twice, to really "see." Here is Joan's response to the photograph of the abandoned truck in the desert. (10 minutes)

Pickup Artist

Headlights—melancholy eyes—
Stare from their metal casing, still.
I return her gaze, but, sadly, I
See longing in her rusty grille.
Once she was new; she roared and thrilled
To scenic rides, cross-country jaunts.
The oil was checked, the gas tank filled,
She ferried me to favorite haunts.
Long years of weather have created
Pits and dents and surface dull;
The roars and thrills have now abated,
And memories hide in her silent hull.
Her shiny metal has turned to rust,
The honey paint disintegrates.
She sits and crumbles in the dust.
She sits, and dying, waits, and waits.

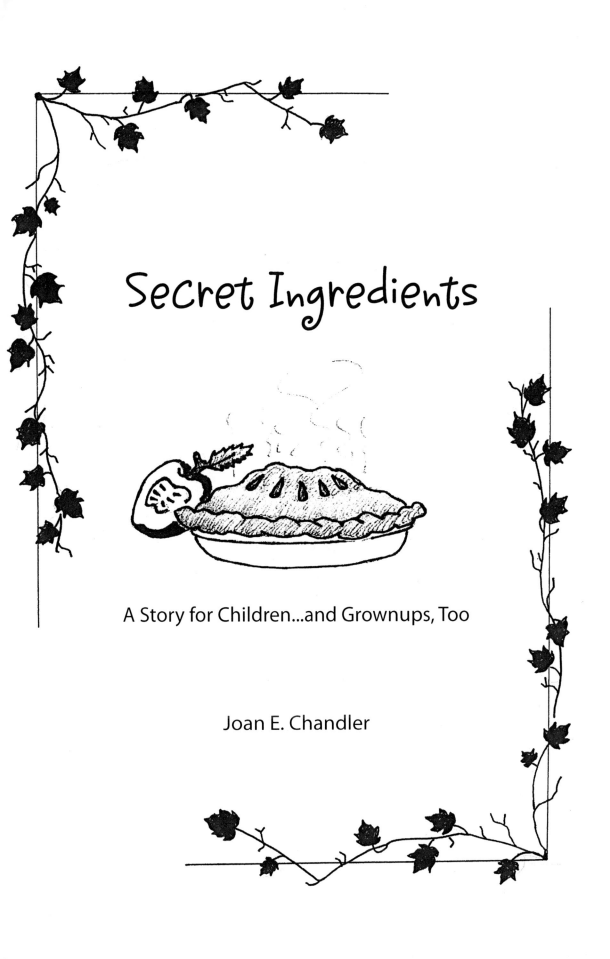

Secret Ingredients

A Story for Children...and Grownups, Too

Joan E. Chandler

To friends who inspired

Bunny's tale

"What a cool, fall day!" said Bunny.

"It is a perfect day to make an apple pie!" Bunny placed Mama's recipe on the counter and began to assemble her pie.

Mama Bunny had always made a simple pie with fresh apples, sugar, flour, and cinnamon.

Bunny put her pie in the oven, then cleaned the table and washed dishes while the pie baked.

"Oh, that smells so spicy and sweet," she said.

While her freshly-baked pie was cooling on the window sill, Bunny went for a walk in the woods. By a huge oak tree, she met Squirrel.

"I just baked a fine apple pie," said Bunny with a smile.

"My Nana makes the best apple pie," said Squirrel. "She adds a *secret ingredient* — two spoonfuls of HONEY."

"Hm," thought Bunny. "That's a good idea. I like Mama's apple pie, but I'm going to make another pie. And this time I'm going to add two spoonfuls of honey."

And she did. And it was a very good pie.

"I made a nice apple pie. It has honey in it," Bunny told her friend, Jay.

"Hey, that sounds good," said Jay. "But I use a *secret ingredient* to make *my* apple pie even better. It's a ripe PEAR."

"Hm," thought Bunny. I like Mama's apple pie, but maybe I'll try adding two spoonfuls of honey and a juicy pear to my next apple pie."

And she did. And it was a very yummy pie.

"Good morning, Buck," said Bunny to her dear deer friend. "I have just made an apple pie. It tastes extra good because I added some honey *and* a pear!"

Buck replied, "My, that does sound wonderful. However, I make the best apple pie, you know, because of a *secret ingredient* — a little VANILLA."

"Hm," Bunny said to herself. "I like Mama's apple pie, but I think I'll put honey and a pear and a spoonful of vanilla in the next pie."

And she did. And of course, the pie was scrumptious.

"Oh, Goose," Bunny said. "Have you heard about my famous apple pie? I put honey, a pear, and some vanilla in it."

Goose smiled. "That sounds quite tasty. But this goose is getting fat! I add a *secret ingredient*—pretend sugar instead of real sugar. And I use only a crust on the BOTTOM, no crust on the top."

"Hm," thought Bunny. "I like Mama's apple pie, but I'll try those ideas as well." And she did.

Bunny invited her friends to sample her latest pie, which she called *Bunny's One Crust Sugar-Free Apple Pear Honey Vanilla Spice Pie.*

"I can taste the honey," said Squirrel.

"I can taste the pear," said Jay.

"I can taste the vanilla," said Buck.

"The pretend sugar makes the pie very sweet," said Goose. "It's quite delicious, even without a crust on top."

 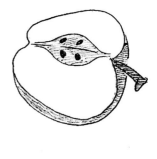

"Hm," thought Bunny. "I wonder if anyone can taste the APPLES."

Bunny couldn't decide which pie she liked better: Mama Bunny's simple apple pie or the one filled with *secret ingredients*.

"Hm," she said. "Sometimes it is fun to try something new. But sometimes the old way is best."

Hmmm. Which apple pie will *you* like best?

Mama Bunny's Apple Pie

8-10 McIntosh or other baking apples   2 tsp. cinnamon
3/4 cup sugar   1 tsp. nutmeg
4 T. flour   Double pie crust

Pare and slice apples. Place in a bowl and toss with dry ingredients. Roll out bottom crust and put in a pie pan. Add apple mixture. Top with another crust, using a fork to crimp the crusts together. Brush with a little milk. Cut holes in top crust with fork tines or sharp knife. Bake at 425 for 10 minutes, then at 350 for about 1 hour.

Bunny's One-Crust Sugar-Free Apple Pear Honey Vanilla Spice Pie

8-10 baking apples   1 Bartlett pear   3 T. flour
½ cup Splenda   2 T. honey   2 tsp. cinnamon
                       Single pie crust

Pare and slice apples and pear. Place in a bowl and toss with dry ingredients. Mix honey and vanilla, and add to apple mixture, tossing thoroughly to coat. Roll pie crust thin and large, and place crust in pie pan. Pour in apple mixture. Bring the crust up over the edge firmly, overlapping the crust around the edges. You will be able to see the fruit through an opening in the top. Brush crust with a little milk. Bake 1 hour at 350.

AFTERTHOUGHTS

I used to imagine that a writer was someone who typed away at all hours of the day and night, making up wonderful stories, smoking cigarettes, drinking loads of coffee (or whiskey), living a cloistered life. I know better now.

It is in the workshop environment where writers share their enthusiasm for writing and learn from each other in new ways—where they discover that writing is fun!

Writers can meet anywhere: a coffee shop, a living room, the bow of a boat, an olive grove in Tuscany, or the deck of a lakefront cottage. It doesn't really matter where they meet, as long as they are dedicated to creativity and collaboration, and wish to learn and practice writing skills in a supportive, engaging, relaxed environment (it helps if there is a close proximity to food!).

The evolution of this book, from the moment Joan suggested it (thanks to her friend, Pat), to the final printing, has been an amazing journey of creativity, hard work, collaboration, feedback, and revision—mostly revision. Revision means to see again, and if not for that, we would have missed the golden nuggets that were hidden in the rubble of our first drafts.

To learn more about
Words in Play Writing Workshops and Retreats,
visit www.wordsinplay.net. We welcome your feedback.

ACKNOWLEDGMENTS

Deb

I wish to thank all my writers, especially those represented in this anthology, for the joy you have given me; you inspire me. Love to my husband and partner, John, who has stood by me through so much, and Jack, the brightest light in my life.

Helen

Thanks to my five children who made many of my stories possible, to Charlie who enriched my life beyond measure, to Joe Medlicott, my first memoir writing teacher, who started me on this treacherous path, to my husband, John, who has heard and laughed at my stories so many times he could write my book, and to my colleagues at *Words in Play*, who have inspired, encouraged, prodded, aided and abetted in getting me to write, not tell, my memoirs.

Jenny

Thanks to my family and friends for their support. They are my inspiration. Without them, I would have few stories to tell. Thanks, too, to all of the wonderful, creative women in my writing group. We gathered around a table to write, critique, eat, cry, and laugh. We buoyed one another's spirits, and became close friends. Our time together will always be a cherished, bright part of my life. I am proud, and pleased, to have this book filled with our stories as a tribute to this special time, and seven dear and unforgettable friends.

Susan Joy

I would like to thank Our Lord for the gift and the desire to write, my daughter Sophia who pushed me into the care of the most outstanding, nurturing writing coach ever, Deb McKew, my husband, Dale, for his faith and encouragement, and my daughter Marguerite, my most enthusiastic reader. To my comrades in ink, no one has experienced the uplifting support of the writers group more than I—you made the difference.

ACKNOWLEDGMENTS

Sally

I raise my glass to Deb and the gals who published here in this anthology. Here's to my family and friends, as well as to the enthusiastic throng following my trials and tribulations on my blog, and to those who avoid it, motivating me to keep trying. And finally, to Stephen Lee, my main guy, my unwavering companion, who keeps me sane on the dreariest of writing days, and who never says no to a party or a challenge, thank you for all you do.

Bobbi

I so valued advice from my writing teachers and others who encouraged me along my way: Miss Faith of Sea Pines School ("You will find your voice in the ocean and the wind."); Miss English of Winsor School, who assigned long, difficult, wonderful books to read over the summers ("Seek only the best metaphor."); and Deb McKew ("Here's another challenge for you!"). Most of all, I thank my sons, Bill, John, and Adam ("Mom, you can do it!") and my grandchildren, who asked "What was your life like so long ago, Grandma?" and who are now already accomplished writers themselves. You make me so proud!

Trudy

Everyone I wish to thank already has her name listed in this book. But, they are definitely worth repeating: Deb McKew, Helen Bridge, Joan Chandler, Sally Wright, Susan Bellavance, Bobbi Stoneman, and Jenny Menning—all strong, creative women with many good stories left to tell.

Joan

Two years ago, my walking buddy, Pat Adams, said to me at breakfast, "Your writing class ought to get together and publish a book." She deserves a big thanks for that spark. Thank you also to my family and friends, who encourage my writing; they also provide adventures and philosophies for me to write about. And to Deb, Sally, Trudy, Helen, Susan, Bobbi, and Jenny: You are imaginative and gifted writers who have become treasured friends.

Breinigsville, PA USA
18 February 2011
255783BV00003B/1/P